AN INTRODUCTION TO
OCTAVIO PAZ

AN INTRODUCTION TO
OCTAVIO PAZ

Alberto Ruy Sánchez

Translated by Jeannine Marie Pitas

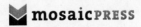

Library and Archives Canada Cataloguing in Publication

Ruy Sánchez, Alberto, 1951-
[Introducción a Octavio Paz. English]
    An introduction to Octavio Paz / Alberto Ruy Sánchez; Jeannine Marie Pitas, translator.

Translation of: Una introducción a Octavio Paz.
Issued in print and electronic formats.
ISBN 978-1-77161-150-3 (softcover).--ISBN 978-1-77161-151-0 (HTML).--
ISBN 978-1-77161-152-7 (Kindle)

1. Paz, Octavio, 1914-1998. 2. Paz, Octavio, 1914-1998--Criticism and interpretation. I. Pitas, Jeannine Marie, translator II. Title. III. Title: Introducción a Octavio Paz. English.

PQ7297.P285Z96213 2018   861'.62   C2018-900960-8
                                             C2018-900961-6

Published by Mosaic Press, Oakville, Ontario, Canada, 2018.
MOSAIC PRESS, Publishers

Una Introducción a Octavio Paz, Alberto Ruy Sánchez Copyright © 2013, Fondo de Cultura Económica, All rights reserved. Mexico D. F.
Translation copyright © 2018, Mosaic Press and Jeannine Marie Pitas
First Spanish-language edition published, 1990 (Joaquín Mortiz).
Revised and expanded Spanish-language edition, 2013 (Fondo Cultura Económica).
Interior design by Courtney Blok

Printed and Bound in Canada

ONTARIO ARTS COUNCIL
CONSEIL DES ARTS DE L'ONTARIO
an Ontario government agency
un organisme du gouvernement de l'Ontario

We acknowledge the Ontario Arts Council
for their support of our publishing program

We acknowledge the Ontario Media Development Corporation
for their support of our publishing program

Funded by the   Financé par le
Government   gouvernement   **Canadä**
of Canada   du Canada

MOSAIC PRESS
1252 Speers Road, Units 1 & 2
Oakville, Ontario L6L 5N9
phone: (905) 825-2130

info@mosaic-press.com

For Anne Husson and François Vitrani,
for Maricarmen Castro and Alfonso Alfaro

TABLE OF CONTENTS

TRANSLATOR'S NOTE

An Introduction to Octavio Paz by Alberto Ruy Sánchez is the most intricate, challenging text I have set out to translate thus far. Combining criticism, literary biography, and a eulogy to a beloved friend and mentor, Alberto Ruy Sánchez has written a beautifully poetic homage to a twentieth-century global literary luminary. Working on this text gave me a new appreciation for Paz's genius and introduced me to the dazzling poesis of Ruy Sánchez himself, who is one of the foremost Mexican writers working today.

Translation, which Gayatri Chakravorty Spivak famously called "the most intimate act of reading," is never a simple task. For me, it is like navigating a difficult sea passage between the Scylla of literalism and the Charybdis of excessive creative license. At times, I am a little too eager to normalize the Spanish text, to make it sound as if it were written originally in English. Lately, I have been striving to stay closer to the original, letting it make my own language somewhat "foreign to itself," as Walter Benjamin would say.

Every so often, I experience moments of disjuncture, when suddenly, I find myself face to face with language that refuses to easily slip into a new code of meaning. For me, these moments are actually some of the most rewarding, as they serve as reminders that the human tendency toward storytelling and meaning-making is incredibly rich and complex, that no one language can ever capture the totality of human reality, and that, no matter how much we think we know, our knowledge will always have limits.

One such moment came when, reading this text, I encountered the title *Libertad bajo palabra*, a 1949 book that Ruy Sánchez considers to be Paz's first significant publication. In Spanish, the term, which literally translates as "freedom under word," refers to parole, but clearly for Paz – and Ruy Sánchez – it means much more, suggesting the limited freedom of the poet as a creator working within the constraints of language. "In the same way, the freedom of poetry has to flow between precise and often limiting verbal forms in order to exist. Poetry is precisely like human existence: conditional freedom, freedom *bajo palabra*," explains Ruy Sánchez when discussing this work (page 55).

There are a few other moments in the text that were perhaps not quite so dazzlingly strange, but where some further context might benefit the reader. Costumbrism, referenced on page 18, was a nineteenth century literary movement in the Spanish-speaking world that combined elements of realism and romanticism, usually taking the form of novels.

"Chingada" (page 68) is a Mexican word with a long history and complex cultural significance. It's a vulgar word but carries a different meaning than its literal counterparts in English, its most famous reference being to La Malinche, the Aztec woman who served as interpreter for Hernando Cortés and has since been viewed as a traitor – and yet, just as Eve is the "mother of all the living," she is one of the mother figures for the Mexican people. Paz has an extensive analysis of this word in *El laberinto de la soledad (The Labyrinth of Solitude)*.

The Contadora Group (page 108) was an organization that attempted to mediate between the Sandinistas and the Contras during the Nicaraguan Civil War of the 1980s. Paz's support of this group demonstrates his long commitment in the realm of politics to seeking synthesis and a middle way between extremes.

A WARNING

This book has come about due to the necessity, expressed by many people in various arenas, to have a comprehensive but very brief vision of the life and work of Octavio Paz. It's an exercise in synthesis: a limited profile of a complex life and a vast, enthralling body of written work. It is a compressed file of information, not a critical essay. As I have suggested, it is a silhouette that might serve as an introduction to this writer's life and work.

It was written, in its first version, for a dictionary of writers published by Charles Scribner's Sons in New York. Its form, brevity and use of reliable sources from within Paz's work are primarily due to the didactic and synthetic requirements put forward by the publisher. I thus thank Carlos A. Solé, editor of that encyclopedic work, for his urgent interest, dedication and insistence on rigour during the production of this text. One challenge of brevity and didactic discipline that seemed especially interesting to me was to consider that these limitations might just be this book's strength: from its first edition in English followed by the one in Spanish and other languages, it has served students and teachers in an academic setting as well as anyone interested in learning about some of the essential keys to Octavio Paz's work. This new edition was edited and expanded up to the time of the poet's death. However, it remains true to the demands of brevity, synthesis of information, and restraint in its use of outside sources and opinions. These include the hundreds – truly hundreds – of people associated with Paz in various countries and contexts – people not mentioned here. I apologize for this in advance. Likewise, I have avoided footnotes to help the reading flow better. A minimal bibliography at the end is the source of assertions and quotations, except for those mentioned directly in the text. It does not include books on Paz even though there are more good, interesting ones published each year. If you are curious to learn more about those, I will refer you to Hugo J. Verani's *Bibliografía crítica (Critical Bibliography)*, which is indispensable.

This book is enhanced by various interviews I did with Octavio Paz, especially those published in the journal *Artes de México (Arts of Mexico)* and for the television series *México en la Obra de Octavio Paz (Mexico in the Work of Octavio Paz)*. At the same time, these pages cannot help but be imbued with the daily proximity that I shared with Octavio Paz over many years through my editorial work and later in our friendship. It is a short way of sharing the privilege of having watched his work become illuminated by his presence. Therefore, although these words try not to make it obvious, they contain – in a discreet way, nearly always unstated - my testimony alongside the readings and daily conversations with Paz's wife Marie José and above all with the writer himself. Nevertheless, he cannot be held responsible for anything said here because he did not see this book until it was printed. His voice is naturally present in my deliberate attempt at synthesis, but not his eyes. For this reason I have to invoke the formula so often stated in these cases: all responsibility is mine. The possible virtues of this book belong to others, especially the author whose words are revealed. The flaws are all mine.

This book was recognized in 1991 with the Premio Binacional de Literatura José Fuentes Mares, (José Fuentes Mares Binational Prize for Literature) given by New Mexico State University at Las Cruces along with the Universidad Autónoma de Ciudad Juárez. It also received a recognition from the Guggenheim Foundation in New York.

I have divided the stream of this "very concise intellectu-al life of Octavio Paz" into five vital circles that follow a time-line. But before this I have wanted to open this new edition by bringing forward a key to the entire work of Octavio Paz, a seed and key to all his writings (including those on history and politics) and his way of being in the world; his conception of poetry as revelation and lucidity, knowledge and action, an act of creation that does not turn its back on history but dwells within it. There is a nut within the nut that is this book: a vi-sion of poetry as a lucid fruit.

After this I approach each period of his life as a collage, looking at the poems and other texts by Octavio Paz. And I mention facts from the poet's life to better understand the work - but not to explain it or simplify its meaning. A writer's life and work are not mirrors of each other as some simple minds would have it. The threads that join life and work are always subtle and complex.

The first chronological circle is one of earth: it is the foun-dation of Paz's territory. It shows the emergence of the artist, his family background and the discovery of his identity as a poet. This circle goes from his birth to his departure from his country: from 1914 through 1943. It covers the first cycle of his poetry.

The second circle is one of air: his first flight outside Mex-ico, his passage through the US, and his residency in postwar France; his encounters with North American poetry and the final phase of surrealism. Also, his productive first return to Mexico. This part goes from 1944 through 1958.

The third circle is one of fire. It is brief and radically trans-formative in his life as much as in his work. It includes the next departure from his country to live in many others, with his life's culminating parentheses in India. It goes from 1959 through 1970.

The fourth circle is of water: swimming against the current, he defies the river of his time. Favourable and unfavourable tides; no lack of storms. This part goes from his return to Mexico in 1971 to his receipt of the Nobel Prize in 1990.

In the fifth circle the movement becomes a spiral. It turns back on itself yet nevertheless keeps moving forward. The central concern is to signal meaning and bring coherence to the retrospective sum total of the work. It is a search for quintessence, for coherence within its diversity. This is the time when Octavio Paz was an editor; that is to say, the builder of the house of his work. He gives it a new foundation. This spiral goes from 1990 to his death in 1998.

These five strokes offer a composite image, similar to that of an artist drawing the outline of a forest; perhaps those who share his vision might feel the temptation to immerse themselves in that forest, to touch the trees that can be seen from a distance, moved by the wind.

It is evident that this book cannot and should not be thought of as a substitution, however slight, for what Octavio Paz himself has written. Instead, it is a very brief invitation to you to read his work.

I. Seed
Lucidity: The Key to the Poem

From the first poems that Octavio Paz recognizes completely as his own – those that opened *Libertad bajo palabra* in 1935 – to the last poem he published in 1996, they all share an unusual common feature. They are separated by more than sixty years as well as many experimentations, mutations and discoveries, in the poet's life as much as in his work. But they are joined by the same notion of the poet as a witness to the fleeting epiphany of life: the sudden apparition of a clarity that vanishes one instant later. And the poem is a language for this exceptional moment in which "thought sees, while eyes think" as life continues its journey toward silence. For Paz, the poet moves through the world with an exceptional degree of lucidity.

Octavio Paz subtitled his final poem "Diálogo con Francisco de Quevedo" ("A Dialogue with Francisco de Quevedo"). But in his first youthful reflections on poetry there was already an indirect dialogue with Quevedo. This was especially true in "Lágrimas de un penitente" ("Tears of a Penitent") in which Paz saw a kind of existentialism *avant la lettre* and also an early breath of Baudelaire, with the idea of having been born in a state of evil with no chance at salvation. In Quevedo, Paz identifies the seed of modern angst and rebellion.

Between the day "made of time and emptiness" that in 1939 appears filled with light and nothingness, and the time and space that in 1996 "fall dizzyingly toward silence," we can observe one of the most singular poetic adventures of the twentieth century.

As a young writer Octavio Paz found himself torn between a purist poetry (which was upheld by the previous generation of poets, whom Paz admired) and a socially engaged poetry (in accord with the messianic idea of a future society that Paz believed was being forged in Latin America). As neither of these two poetic approaches left him completely satisfied, he began to formulate a paradoxical solution: the poem as a black light calling for an awareness of being in the world, of living among others and inside of history. The poem as a synthesis of opposites: the bow of the warrior and the lyre of the singer. Neither opposed nor subordinated to history, the poet burns with the passionate awareness of moving within it.

However, the poem is also the deepest presence of life, its miracles and disasters. A perpetual search: "And I dive into life and grasp at nothing." Meanwhile, a ritual search for the body of the beloved: "singular land that I know, that knows me, the only nation I believe in, the only door to the infinite."

In this way, the poetry of Paz is forged between the abyss of existential solitude and a transcendent communion with others, especially the beloved: "Beyond us, at the border between change and constancy, a life more alive comes to claim us."

In the postwar era Paz lived in Paris and was drawn to surrealism. "It was a group of free poets in a city intoxicated by theories and ideologies that heightened the passions but did not illuminate the soul." The prose poems of *Águila o sol?* (*Eagle or Sun?*) bear a trace of this fascination. And the long poem *Piedra del Sol* (*Sunstone*), from 1957, a centrepiece of Paz's work, is a synthesis of all his concerns up to that point. A crucible of his formal explorations and poetic thought. Abyss and erotism, history and personal memory, symbol and material, sensation and idea, all come together at last in a poetic form that is an echo of tradition and a challenge to that same tradition. A summation and rebirth of the poet.

Later, starting in 1962 in India, his poetry convulses and a protracted erotism becomes the cornerstone of his search.

The encounter with Marie José Paz, from whom he would not separate for a single day from 1964 to his death in 1998, marks this new way of being: "Sometimes poetry is the frenzy of bodies and the frenzy of delight and the frenzy of death." His poetry becomes an expression of erotism.

The long poem *Blanco* (*White*) and the narrative poem *El mono gramático* (*The Grammarian Monkey*) synthesized the double trace of otherness in his world: that of the Orient and that of his beloved. But all too soon, an expulsion from paradise would occur. A poem on the murder of students in Mexico in 1968 would accompany his refusal to serve as an ambassador of the government responsible for that crime. This gesture would be remembered upon his receipt of the Nobel Prize in 1990.

In "Nocturno de San Ildefonso" ("San Ildefonso Nocturne") as well as "Pasado en claro"("A Draft of Shadows") and other poems from the 70's, we see a rebirth of his concerns for personal memory interlaced with history. Paz reformulates his poetic solution, giving poetry the function of greatest lucidity.

Poetry is a critique of modernity – in the realm of the passions rather than the intellect, in the name of realities denied by the modern age. It is what Octavio Paz calls "the other voice": that of the human who sleeps in the background of every human. The one who, through poetry, is not explained or analyzed but revealed, evoked and inspired. Poetry is fed by the imagination and is, according to Paz, "the antidote to technology and the market," those new empty idols of the masses, which replaced the previous ones: religious dogmas and totalitarian ideologies.

Octavio Paz wrote many fundamental essays on art, society, history, international politics and Mexican politics; with these his work already forms a cornerstone of contemporary culture. But it is his poetry that contains this lucid axis that nourished his thought and his peculiar way of being in the world. The poetry is the master key to his oeuvre as a whole.

Thus, those who comment on his political ideas without understanding the poetic rebellion that underlies them only
understand the shadow of what he is saying. Octavio Paz is
faithful to a reading of Aristotle's poetics that makes a radical
distinction between the historian and the poet. The first writes
what happened; the second questions what happened with a
wider vision that does not conform to what others think and
say, considering instead what should have happened and what
could have happened. The poet's vision, wider, with more dimensions (including sensory ones), more unsettled and unsettling, forms a foundation for his political essays as well as
his writings on art.

His last poem, a final dialogue with Quevedo, seeks to be a
poem of reconciliation with life's fragility, its convulsions and
abysses. Paz has stated that this is something only T. S. Eliot
actually achieved. Life returns to silence, to the death of the
poet, but this does not matter because "we already know that
music is silence and we are one chord in the concert." Thus I
begin at the end and begin again.

II
Circle of Earth
The Emergence of the Poet: 1914-1943

1. Poetics as Territory

Toward the end of the 1930's, a new generation of writers appeared on the Mexican cultural scene. They were associated with the magazine *Taller* (*Workshop*). Their presence was notorious because they showed, with a certain violence from their first expressions, a new awareness and a new attitude toward literature and the world. Their main difference from the previous generation might be defined precisely in their conception of the special place that poetic work occupies in the movements of history: neither indifferent nor subordinate to it. Literary creation could not decidedly turn its back on all the occurrences and political and social movements that characterized this generation's time, but neither was it an automatic transmission of those same historic events. They held neither to simple "social" poetry nor innocently "pure" poetry, but rather a new, richer, less schematic conception of poetry. They did not reach this idea without conflicts and contradictions between certain political ideas and their aesthetic sensibility. They frequently tried out different poetic paths.

Also, as these poets were the natural heirs to thirty years of artistic avant gardes throughout the world, it was possible for them to seek and find new poetic forms to suit their new search for meaning. And that was the meaning of their experimentation, as these young voices offered a truly new song that tried not merely to reproduce what they called "rhetoric," which Octavio Paz poetically criticized thus:

The birds sing, they sing
but don't know what they're singing:
their only understanding is their throat.

This new awareness would give a face, through many books
over a period of many years, to a large part of Mexican literary
culture, at least for the next seven decades. They would initi-
ate a literary period that perhaps has not ended. The values,
explorations, motives, and poetic usage of these writers were
in large measure those that, toward the end of the century,
became the face of Mexican literature, and this will probably
continue to be the case for some time. However, the poets of
this Mexican generation, alongside other poets of the same
generation in other Latin American countries as well as Spain,
were initiating the change toward what was destined to become the modern poetry of Hispanic America.

Octavio Paz was among those young writers who were
under thirty at the beginning of the 1940's. Especially active,
belligerent, and productive in his creation of poetry, essays,
translation and criticism, Paz would clearly become the pro-
tagonist of his generation and the literary period that this generation initiated.

What is the alchemy of this poet? The familial, social, and
political ingredients, combined with the transforming fire of
his person, make him the unique poet he was. The relationship
between life and work is always more complex than it seems.
The life gives indications of the rare creation that makes up
the work of an innovative poet. But biography never explains
a work completely. Likewise, the work does not explain the
life. Both of these, insufficient as mutual support, weave a singular, unique story. A kind of third reality. And this pulses in
the imagination of readers who establish the bridge between
what this author lived and wrote. To observe and try to com-
prehend the transformative alchemy of the life and work of a

poet is always an adventure and a search. It is to recognize that there is a mystery, to follow the clues toward solving it but also to accept that some aspect of the mystery remains. Here and there along this road the keys to the work become evident, as does the pleasure of coming to understand it.

2. Learning To Sing, Face To The Wind

Octavio Paz Lozano was born in Mexico City on March 31, 1914. The father's side of his family had its origins in Jalisco (his grandfather Ireneo) and Colima (his grandmother Rosa), and the mother's side was of Andalucian origin (his maternal grandfather was from Medina-Sidonia and his grandmother was from Puerto de Santa María). There is a mythical portrait of his mother Josefina Lozano, born in Mexico, in his poem "Pasado en claro," ("A Draft of Shadows") written many years after her death. This poem also describes the family environment and the grandfather Ireneo's mansion.

> They also gave me bread, they gave me time,
> clear in the curves of the days,
> havens where I could be alone with myself.
> A child among quiet adults
> and their terrible childishness,
> a child in the hallways with tall doors
> rooms with portraits,
> twilight guilds of the absent,
> child survivor
> of the mirrors without memory
> and their town of wind:
> time and its incarnations
> turned into a reflection simulacrum.
> In my house the dead were more than the living.
> My mother, a thousand-year-old girl,
> mother of the world, my orphan,

selfless, ferocious, obtuse, foreseeing,
goldfinch, dog, ant, wild sow,
love letter lacking in language,
my mother: the bread that I cut
with her own knife every day.

Ireneo Paz Flores, the poet's paternal grandfather, was a prominent intellectual liberal and Freemason who participated in the great historic occurrences of his century: he was a member of the army that fought the French intervention of Napoleon III in Mexico and reached the rank of colonel; he was government secretary in the state of Sinaloa; he was part of the rebel movement that brought Porfirio Díaz to the presidency of the nation; he was a member of the City Council of Mexico City and a member of the Mexican Congress (Congreso de la Unión). He wrote a biography of Porfirio Díaz, *Vida y muerte del más celebre bandido sonorense Joaquín Murrieta* (*Life and Adventures of the Celebrated Bandit Joaquin Murrieta: His Exploits in the State of California*), various historical novels (*Doña Marina; Amor y suplicio,* or *Love and Anguish; Leyendas históricas de la Independencia,* or *Historical Legends of Independence*); costumbrist novels (*Amor de viejo, or An Old Man's Love; Las dos Antonias,* or *The Two Antonias; La piedra del sacrificio,* or *The Sacrificial Stone*); works of theatre (*La bolsa o la vida,* or *Your Money or Your Life; Los héroes del día siguiente,* or *Heroes of the Day After; La manzana de la discordia,* or *The Apple of Discord*); his volumes of memoir (*Algunas campañas,* or *Some Campaigns*) and also one book of poems (*Cardos y violetas,* or *Thistles and Violets*). He was the owner of a printing company, a publishing house and several newspapers. The last one, *La Patria* (*The Nation*) was set on fire and confiscated by the government of Venustiano Carranza, whom the newspaper had criticized. Ireneo Paz was 78 when Octavio was born – almost the same age (just two years older) than his grandson would be when he won the Nobel Prize.

Thanks to the extensive library of his grandfather, from a young age Octavio Paz was able to read Benito Pérez Galdós, Lope de Vega, Calderón de la Barca, Juan Ruiz de Alarcón, Luis de Góngora, Francisco de Quevedo and many others. All the fundamental poetry of his mother tongue was at his reach in this library, including the work of the Hispanic American "modernista" writers from the end of the nineteenth century and beginning of the twentieth. The French novelists and poets occupied a good part of this great library. There, as a child, he was introduced to literature and all its power by his aunt, Amalia Paz:

> A virgin who talked in her sleep, an aunt
> taught me to see with my eyes closed,
> to look within and through the wall.

With her he would begin his immense exploration of French literature and art; his continuous dialogue with a culture that, in different ways and not only in the twentieth century, left subtle traces in Mexican literature and art. In his text "Mutuas inspiraciones" ("Mutual Inspirations") Paz states the following:

> I belong to a middle class French-influenced Mexican family. Around 1910 there were many such families. What is meant when one speaks of "Frenchification?" If we consult a dictionary we find that the word applies to those who imitate the French in an exaggerated manner. The same is said of those who, in Spain, followed Napoleon's party in the past century. But the word has a fuller, nobler and richer meaning. It's enough to read our historians, novelists and thinkers to confirm that, since the end of the eighteenth century, those associated with the Enlightenment and, later, those who sympathized with the French Revolution were seen as "Frenchified." The word continued to be

used throughout the nineteenth century to designate the liberals. In this sense, nearly all our great liberals were "Frenchified," from José Luis Mora to Ignacio Ramírez, from Altamirano to Justo Sierra. Some admired Benjamin Constant, others Danton; some were Girondins, others Jacobins, still others followers of the First Consul or even the Emperor. By the end of the century the term "Frenchification" acquired an aesthetic color, coming to mean someone who was a symbolist or decadent, a devotee of Flaubert or Zola or, ultimately, as Rubén Darío puts it, "with Hugo, strong, and with Verlaine, ambiguous." In this way we reach the twentieth century, the realism of Azuela and Marín Luis Guzmán, the prose of Reyes and de Torri, the poetry of Tablada, González Martínez, López Velarde, Villaurrutia, Gorostiza, Torres Bodet. The work of all these writers – and they are not the only ones – sustains a dialogue, sometimes open and at other times covert, with French literature.

The poet's grandfather Ireneo Paz died in 1924 at age eighty eight, while he was checking the time - which turned out to be the hour of his death. His grandson, who was ten at the time, was present during that scene and would relive it later in a poem, "Elegia interrumpida" ("Interrupted Elegy"), later included in the section "Puerta condenada, 1938-1946" ("The Condemned Door", 1938-1946) from the book *Libertad bajo palabra*), where the poet recounts his deceased family members and faces their death while also acknowledging its presence inside himself. The book opens with the section dedicated to his grandfather:

> Today I remember the dead of my house.
> We do not forget the first dead man
> though he dies in a flash, so hurriedly

that he does not reach the bed or the oil paintings.
I hear the cane, unsure on the step,
the body that steadies itself with a sigh,
the door that opens, the dead man that enters.
From a door to death there's not much space
and not even time to sit down,
lift his head, check the clock,
and see the time: quarter past eight.

In another poem, "Pasado en claro" ("A Draft of Shadows") the figure of Ireneo Paz appears to offer the child a vital lesson:

The ash trees taught me
under the rain, patience
to sing vehemently facing the wind.
[...] My grandfather smiling when he fell
and repeating at each disaster: "What's done is done.")
(These words are soil scattered over your name:
may they fall softly upon you).

The poet's father studied law and wrote a thesis on freedom of the press. He was an agent of the Public Ministry and a manager of a family printing business that would be looted and burned during the Mexican Revolution. Octavio Paz Solórzano (1883-1936), like his father, was an active political journalist. First he wrote against Zapata, but later he became a fervent supporter of his cause - perhaps under the influence of his friend, the celebrated Antonio Díaz Soto y Gama. He and other progressive intellectuals joined the movement headed by Emiliano Zapata. He participated in the revolutionary Convention when it was moved from Aguascalientes to Mexico City in 1915, and after its general dissolution he participated in the attempt to continue it in the city of Toluca in 1916. From that year he lived in self-imposed exile in the United States until 1920 as a representative and promoter of the image of Zapa-

ta and his Liberation Army. With Ramón Puente he founded
La Semana, a newspaper representing Francisco Villa in exile,
and he tried his luck at various other activities in Los Angeles.

In a decision that her entire family disapproved of, Josefina
decided to follow her husband into exile. Octavio was not even
four years old when he and his mother set off on the long, difficult journey that, as he would later recall, included many long
stops (one of them in Guadalajara) and just generally seemed
like it would have no end. One day, speaking to me of his exile,
Octavio began to recount various images of this journey that
he underwent with much anxiety, dozing for nearly the entire
journey, consumed by the feeling of anxiety that dominated his
mother. This journey was, he later said, "a nightmare without
end." For the poet, the desert became synonymous with the
grief that was building inside his mother, who sensed she was
not going to like whatever situation she found her husband
in. It was a very different reality than the extreme loneliness
he expressed in his letters. According to Octavio, she spoke to
others – relatives and friends – as if engaged in battle, a crusade to win him back. And his father's alcoholism hovered
over his mother like a threatening ghost. Octavio also remembered being teased by other children for not speaking English;
humiliating nicknames were imposed upon him, and he also
experienced disgust at the tastes and smells of his new environment. He and his mother essentially lived alone, as if his
father were working in another city. He spent all his time away
from home. At last they all returned to Mexico. From then on
the relationship between Paz's parents was basically ruined.

Octavio Paz Solórzano was one of the initiators of agrarian
reform and a founder, upon his return from the United States,
of the Partido Nacional Agrarista (National Agrarian Reform
Party). He wrote a passionate biography of Zapata in which
his recounting of historic events was mixed with a fervent defence of agrarian reformers' ideas. It also included an interesting summary of *Estampas de la revolución del sur*. (*Impressions*

from the Revolution of the South.) He died tragically, in 1934, run over by a train. His death would appear in Octavio Paz's poem "Pasado en claro," ("A Draft of Shadows") in which, as the poet himself says, "Death is the mother of shapes" and "the years and the dead and the syllables are different tellings of the same tale."

> From vomit to thirst
> bound to the colt of alcohol
> my father came and went among the flames.
> One evening, among the sleepers and rails
> of a train station filled with flies and dust
> we pieced him back together.
> I never managed to speak with him.
> Now I meet him in dreams,
> that blurred country of the dead.
> We always spoke of other things.
> As the house collapsed
> I grew up. I was (I am) grass, weeds
> among anonymous rubble.

In sum, an impoverished family, a varied, rich, intense intellectual heritage, a house filled with cracks, with portraits of dead relatives and books. And among all this would come an encounter with poetry, with life transformed into poetic images.

The adolescent Octavio Paz, a wandering sixteen-year-old boy who would discover the world on the streets, astonished by all he saw, appears in a memoir poem he would later write in the 1980's: "1930: Vistas fijas" ("1930: Fixed Visions"):

> What or who guided me? I didn't seek anything or anyone;
>   I sought everything and everyone:
> vegetation of blue domes and white bell towers, walls
>   the colour of dried blood, architecture:
> a feast of forms, a petrified dance under the clouds that are

> made and unmade, never cease to be made, always
> moving toward their next becoming [...]
> the parks and plazas, the grave populations of singing
>   poplars and laconic elms, baby sparrows and mockingbirds [...]
> streets that never end, streets people walk on the way they read
>   books or explore a body;

Walking the streets the adolescent enters the houses' courtyards with their hanging birdcages; he sees outdoor markets,
fruit stands and candy stalls, movie posters at cinemas, hand-
made paper decorations hanging in the streets, couples in
love, elders, "branches split off from the tree of the century,"
the music of the market, nightfall, and finally,

> the night populated by murmuring and, there in the distance
>   a murmur of women's voices, blurred foliage
>   moved by the wind [...]
> The couples, forests of feverish columns
>   wrapped in an animal's breath
>   desiring a thousand eyes and a thousand hands and one sole
>   image nailed to their foreheads,
> the calm couples that advance without moving,
>   their eyes closed as they fall
>   endlessly into themselves;
> the motionless vertigo of an exhumed adolescent
>   who breaks through my forehead as I write
> and walks again, superalone in his
>   alonity, through broken streets and plazas
>   I can hardly speak of them
> and he gets lost again in the search for everything and
> everyone, nothing and no one.

Many of the images contained in the rest of the poem come
from popular fiestas, or the Sunday celebrations in the streets
of his town, Mixcoac. From the age of just a few months, Octa-

vio Paz lived in the old section of Mixcoac, which today is a relatively central neighbourhood of Mexico City but at that time was a separate community. When his father joined Zapata and left the city, the young child and his mother took refuge in the grandfather Ireneo's mansion. Returning from their exile in Los Angeles, the Paz family once again lived with him, but in a different, smaller house, three blocks away from the mansion that would continue to be the sentimental core of the child's memories. Ireneo Paz's mansion, now a convent, still stands on the edge of a plaza filled with ash trees and facing a seventeenth century church dedicated to San Juan.

In a "memory exercise" about Mixcoac, "Estrofas para un jardín imaginario" ("Stanzas for an Imaginary Garden") the poet recalls what this devastated town once was and is no longer. But he also evokes one of his first encounters with poetry: "One afternoon, running out from my school, I stopped suddenly; I felt as if I were in the centre of the world. I lifted my eyes and saw, between two clouds, an open blue sky, indecipherable, infinite. I didn't know what to say: I encountered an eagerness and, perhaps, poetry."

In Claudio Isaac's documentary film *El lenguaje de los árboles* (*The Language of the Trees*), Octavio Paz remembers, in the garden of that house in Mixcoac, one of the first definitions of his vocation:

> When I think of my childhood, I think of an old house from the end of the past century located in a town on the outskirts of Mexico City. The house still stands beside the plaza that it shares with another renowned home from the end of the eighteenth century, where Valentín Gómez Farías lived (today it is home to the Instituto Mora [Mora Institute]). This plaza was popular and every year on December 12, feast of Our Lady of Guadalupe, there was a party with vendors and fireworks. My household lacked many things – we were a

family ruined by the Revolution – but we had an abun-
dance of books as well as flowers. There was a garden,
an unkempt, somewhat wild old garden with tall grass
and several trees: ashes and some pines. Among all
these trees my favourite was the fig, which marked
the passage of a year. For six months starting in autumn it was a black skeleton, and then it would turn
green once again. The fruits were also mysterious:
the fig was a fruit-like flower or a flowery fruit. The
skin is black and covers a dark, red flowering. I have
sometimes thought that eating figs is like eating sun,
devouring the night.

My cousins, my friends and I played in that garden,
but I also managed to stay by myself, to climb the fig
tree and, hidden in the foliage, imagine I was navigating through space, exploring it. The fig tree, of course,
did not move one millimetre from the ground, but up
high, on a branch that seemed like the mast of a sailboat, I could see the horizon and the clouds; above all,
I explored all the time. The fig tree was a temptation
toward heroism and action, a mimicry of the heroic.
Nevertheless, I soon realized that I was not destined to
lead an active life; I did not want to be a saint or hero.
Nor did I seek the contemplative life of the philosopher. From my childhood, I felt that I was destined for
a life in letters. I remember being impressed by a story
about Alexander the Great. As a child he was asked if
he would prefer to be Homer the poet or Achilles the
hero. And Alexander the Great replied: you are asking
me if I want to be the trumpet or the hero celebrated
by the trumpet: I want to be Achilles. And he was. But
this response from Alexander was quite perplexing to
me because I wanted to be Homer. Of course, my idea
of poetry was not that of a trumpet; I did not believe

then, or now, that poetry is a trumpet destined to cel-
ebrate the acts, the great deeds of heroes, the mighty
of this world. Poetry also sings of human adversity and
misfortune.

Thus, in 1989 his poetry would sing of the destruction of
Mixcoac, a town that was then completely swallowed by the
expanding metropolis of Mexico City. When Paz was a child,
this town had its own character as a typical small town. In
the pre-Hispanic period it had been a population dedicated to
Mixcóatl, a celestial warrior god that appears drawn in the ancient codexes, his body painted in dark blue with white points
that represent the stars and a black mask that represents the
night sky.

After visiting what remains of the place in which he had
spent his childhood and adolescence, he wrote a poem entitled
"Epitafio sobre ninguna piedra" ("An Epitaph on No Stone"):

> Mixcoac was my town: three nocturnal syllables,
> a shadowy mask over a solar face.
> Our Lady arrived, the mother Dustcloud.
> She came and devoured him. I walked through the world.
> My house was words, my tomb air.

3. Poetic Passion, Social Passion

Octavio Paz's father and grandfather understood and cultivat-
ed with intense emotion both the full silence of the writer as
well and the enthusiastic noise of social action, journalism,
war and politics. Therefore, perhaps it is nothing strange that,
starting in his adolescence during secondary school, Paz revealed himself to be very sensitive to Mexico's social problems
and participated in the student movements of the time. He was
introduced to anarchism by a Catalan classmate, José Bosch,
the son of an old militant of the Federación Anarquista Ibérica

(Iberian Anarchist Federation). The two adolescents shared
reading recommendations with each other: Bosch read novels and poetry; Paz avidly read Kropotkin, Proudhon, Reclus
and Ferrer. Soon after this, both attempted to get their fellow
students from the Escuela Secundaria Número 3 (Secondary
School Number 3) to go on strike. Paz would later recount that
"the principal called the police, closed the school for two days
and brought us to the detention centre of the Inspección de
Policía (Police Inspection Authority). We spent two nights in
jail."

In 1931 he entered the Escuela Nacional Preparatoria (National Preparatory School), located in the building of the old
Colegio de San Ildefonso, which was a great educational in-
stitution of the Jesuits of New Spain, and whose name graces
"Nocturno de San Ildefonso" ("San Ildefonso Nocturne"), the
poem which he wrote invoking the Mexico he knew in 1931
but wrote nearly four decades later. In this poem he reveals
the intensity of that period and criticizes the ways in which social passion was transformed into a passion for violence that
infected the ideals shared by the preparatory school students
of that time.

> The boy who walks through this poem
> between San Ildefonso and el Zócalo,
> is the man who writes it:
> > > this page
> is also a nocturnal stroll.
> > Here friendly ghosts
> assume flesh,
> > ideas vanish.
> The good, we wanted the good:
> > > to set the world right.
> We didn't lack strength
> > we lacked humility.
> What we wanted, we didn't want innocently.

Precepts and concepts,
    the arrogance of theologians
to strike others with the cross
        to lay foundations of blood
to build a house from bricks of crime
to order obligatory communion.

But if Paz's social concern and political passion continued alive and militant, his poetic passion kept on maturing along other roads that sometimes ran parallel and at other times moved in an opposite direction. During the years he spent in the preparatory school he personally met the most important poets of the prior generation, and he became immersed in the poetry of his age. Carlos Pellicer, José Gorostiza and the Mexicanist philosopher Samuel Ramos were his teachers. He also met Jorge Cuesta and Xavier Villaurrutia, who appreciated him greatly. A celebrated anthology of poetry by Gerardo Diego was his surprising port of entry into the Spanish poetry scene; an anthology by Jorge Cuesta was his entry into the Mexican one.

At that time, along with Salvador Toscano, José Alvarado, Rafael López Malo, and Arnulfo Martínez Lavalle, he founded his first journal, *Barandal* (1931-1932). Here, his generation encountered the century's literary avant gardes. Here Paz published his first essay, "Ethics of the artist," a reflection on the testimonial and historical value of art. With the same friends he would later edit a second journal, *Cuadernos del Valle de México* (*Notebooks from the Valley of Mexico*) (1933-1934), which was important because its contributors began to formulate a little more clearly the need to go beyond what they called "pure poetry."

Nevertheless, in that moment Paz published a kind of poetry that his contemporaries disparaged with the term "intimist." And his first book, *Luna silvestre* (*Wild Moon*), published in 1933, contains not the slightest allusion to history or politics.

In 1934, Rafael Alberti came to Mexico.

> This was the first time – said Octavio Paz – that I heard a poet recite his poems in public, and I was dazzled. Alberti was already a member of the Spanish Communist Party, and he was visiting America on a propaganda tour. He gave several lectures and read his poems. The lectures weren't so memorable, but the poetry readings impressed me. It was a great revelation for me. After his public appearances, sometimes we met in a bar and stayed up talking until three or four in the morning, Spanish style. One night, we all read him our poems. How generous Alberti was with us. We were all on the left, but at that time I was feeling a certain mistrust toward political poetry and any literature that was described as "committed." At that time, Alberti wrote political poetry. It was the period of *Consignas* (*Slogans*), that little book which asserted that poetry should be at the service of the Communist Party.
>
> Reading the poems of this twenty-year-old man, Alberti stated that this was not explicitly a political or social poetry, but it was more "revolutionary" than the others due to its determination to transform language itself.

In 1937, at age twenty-three, Paz decided simultaneously to leave his family home, his university law program, and Mexico City. He spent nearly four months in the Southeast of the country, in Yucatán, involved with various friends, among them Octavio Novaro, in teaching at a new progressive school for workers. He had already done this years earlier in Mexico City, when he was a member of an organization called the Unión de Estudiantes Pro Obreros y Campesinos) (Union of Students Pro-Workers and Farmers), which opened night schools around the city - schools whose classes quickly turned into political meetings.

In May 1937 he published in *El Nacional* (*The National*), a Mexico City newspaper, the "Notes" from his journey from Mérida. In these writings his poetic impressions of the place and its people are combined with his social conscience, all of it coloured with a good dose of utopia. The strong indigenous presence in Yucatán was highly moving for the poet. According to the young author, this presence along with the strikes and meetings of farmers and workers in Mérida, "dignifies and reveals the truth" of a city reclaimed by the country. He also does not fail to perceive the sensual heartbeat of the city, its erotic dimension:

> At night the city pants; hanging out in the balconies or doorways, the young girls converse, and their voices are like those of a deep river, the dark foreboding of water. Sometimes a weather vane moans deafly. A tumult of iron and stone and a penetrating smell of lips and sweaty members grows in a silent street; a carriage passes by. At these hours there is, despite the breeze pushing the nearby sea, a distress that oppresses and captivates; one can sense a hidden, enclosed sexual life, contained, furiously secret and restrained.

The author reclaims the conservation and the strength of the Mayan presence on the peninsula. He attacks imperialism, the large landowners, the spirit of classism. Finally, he finds a symbol of life and death in Yucatán: the henequen plant. "Here, as in all the capitalist regime, man lives by the death of man. Sometimes, at night, one awakens as if on rubble and blood. The henequen, invisible and quotidian, presides over this waking."

This was, in Mexico, the period of the populist government of the president Lázaro Cárdenas, a time of agrarian reform and large mass movements. Impressed by the poverty of the

Mayan peasants devoted to the cultivation of henequen, he wrote the first version of his poem "Entre la piedra y la flor" ("Between the Stone and the Flower"). In this he tried to show the contrast between the simple, ritual life of those peasants and the abstract, global system of money that oppressed their existence without them even knowing it. Between the stone and the flower, between the harsh aridity of that land and the breathtaking agave flower, the poet encounters humanity. Like a stubborn rain falling on stones, human beings and their works appear.

Apart from the author's social intentions, there lies in this poem, from its very first version, an appropriate, fortunate expression of the life it recreates. There lies in it a kind of deep truth that is preserved beyond the political interpretation that animates it. Considered by the author, after several revisions, as a relatively failed or at least unsatisfactory attempt, this poem is in any case a clear testimony to one aspect of Octavio Paz's poetic concerns during those years. A minor gradient, for certain. But "Entre la piedra y la flor"("Between the Stone and the Flower") was not so evidently a "social poem" as another that Paz published separately, in 1936, about the Spanish Civil War. "¡No pasarán!" ("They Shall Not Pass!") written with a rhetoric that the author would later reject completely. The earnings from the sale of this poem were destined for the Frente Popular Español en México (Spanish Popular Front in Mexico).

Both social poems form a very clear contrast to the ones included in Octavio Paz's two first books, *Luna silvestre* (*Wild Moon*) in 1933 and *Raíz del hombre* (*Root of Man*) in 1937. In the first of these we see an attempt to unite intellectual rigor with lyricism. In both books erotic love poetry occupies a central place; the direction that all his poetry would take that has its origin in these two volumes.

The seven poems of *La luna silvestre* (*Wild Moon*) would, with time, be rejected by their author and removed from his later anthologies, only to reappear in *Obras completas* (*Complete Works*). Nevertheless, in one of these, the fifth of the brief volume, we already see a sign of the passionate vein his poetry would explore frequently: words as an emanation of desire, a bridge between bodies, a powerful invocation of the beloved.

> In the silence, your words
> still resounding;
>
> under the branches, your words falling
> like a slow wooden light.
>
> My arms surrounding the perfect circle,
> the space filled with memories
> left by the absence of your body.
>
> Here, distant one, you are always present,
> hazy, like a turbid childhood memory.

Luna silvestre (*Wild Moon*), still signed by the author with his two surnames (Octavio Paz Lozano), never received any commentary. But his next books received very contrasting reviews. Under the pseudonym of Marcial Rojas, Bernardo Ortiz de Montellano published the first written commentary on Octavio Paz's poetry – a negative review. In an article entitled "Retórica y poesía" ("Rhetoric and Poetry") published in the biweekly *Letras de México* (*Mexican Letters*), number I, 15 in January 1937), without even mentioning the poet's name, Marcial Rojas cited his social poetry, asserting that it did not actually qualify as poetry.

But while "¡No pasarán!" ("They Shall Not Pass") was considered a work of eminently "progressive" rhetoric, *Raíz del hombre* (*Root of Man*) was received as a book of real quality that had been expected by this talented young man. The poet and essayist Jorge Cuesta was the first to write about Octavio Paz regarding this book: *Letras de México* (*Mexican Letter*, no.2, 1 February 1937):

> What drew my attention to Octavio Paz during his youth was the decisiveness and wilfulness with which he was able to expose his guts to the voracity of the object [...] And I was waiting for a book of his, like *Raíz del hombre* (*Root of Man*), to confirm in his poetry a command of his own destiny. Now I am certain that Octavio Paz has a future. By now he cannot free himself from having provoked it and made it manifest to us [...] The voices of López Velarde, Carlos Pellicer, Xavier Villaurrutia, and Pablo Neruda are unmistakeable; they resound in the poems of Paz [...] Their presence in the poetry of Octavio Paz offers them the most secure and worthwhile future that might be given to them.

The incisive note by Jorge Cuesta led the poet to be introduced the celebrated Contemporáneos (Contemporaries) group, with Cuesta and Villaurrutia as godfathers, at a meal where, among other topics, they discussed what they saw as the contradiction between Paz's political ideas and his poetry.

The same year, during his stay in Yucatán, a region with important archaeological zones, he discovered the richness of Mexico's prehispanic past and briefly expressed the desire to become an archaeologist. That fascination – love, horror, passionate curiosity – with the ancient world of Mexico would be fundamental to his work as a poet and an essayist. His later works on prehispanic Mexico – especially its art – would come to be indispensable, even for specialists. "The art of Mexico bewitched me," he would later say in an interview. At times it seems like a terrible art. At times it seems like an art that opens the door to another reality and another dimension of our consciousness.

4. Questions of Time

In 1937, for Octavio Paz time is a code for a thousand questions and demands. Time is the History that requires humans to reach its own level. Faced with the Spanish Civil War, Octavio Paz responded actively; he served the Spanish Republic from Mexico in various associations; he wrote, as we have already said, the famous poem "¡No pasarán!"("They Shall Not Pass!") and offered its royalties to the cause; in Yucatán he founded the Comité Pro Democracia Española (The Pro Spanish Democracy Committee), and he also participated in the workers' schools.

Time is also the history of poetry, demanding that the young poet offer forms to fit his or her vital moment. Time is also time of the poem: wilfulness of form. Time is the ritual time of words. Time is the encounter with the beloved, her erotic evocation and invocation. Thus, *Raíz del hombre* (*Root of Man*) the book that Jorge Cuesta commented on enthusiastically, is another response to what he saw as the demands of time. In its first edition, it included fifteen poems and an introduction. The last edition contains only three of those poems, with modifications. In its time it was the first long poem of Octavio Paz, perhaps constructed with less compositional rigor than his other long poems, or at least with less awareness of the nature of a long poem. This is a theme that in time would profoundly interest the poet, as much in practice (as he would come to write at least ten poems in this genre) as well as in theory and criticism (as he would later give lectures and write important essays on the long poem).

The erotism in *Raíz del hombre* (*Root of Man*) is an abyss in which man suddenly finds himself face to face with his biological and total history. In the instant of encounter with the beloved, the past and future, life, love and death coincide:

Stretched out and torn,

to the right of my veins, mute;
infinite on mortal shores,
mortal and serpentine.

I touch your delirious surface,
the silent, panting pores,
the circular course of your blood,
its repeated pulsing, green and tepid.

First comes a dawning relief,
a soft presence of throbbings
that cross your skin, all lips
resplendent touch of caresses.

[...]

Thrown in white spirals
we scrape against our origin and roots;
ages, dreams, times turn backwards;
the vegetation calls to us,
the stone remembers us
and the thirsting root
of the tree that grew from our dust.

I discern your face among the shadows,
the terrible weeping of your sex,
your intimacy life's nothingness,
sensing the origin of your relief
and the death you carry, hidden

Children, shadows navigate through your eyes,
lightning bolts, my eyes, the void.

The passionate poet saw in woman a code to humanity's deep
time. He also saw it in the henequen plant ("Entre la piedra y

la flor" "Between the Stone and the Flower"), a code for the human time of ritual work that has been exploited; in others words, a code of life and death.

> The henequen
> a green geometry lesson
> upon the white and ochre earth,
> farming, commerce, industry, language.
> It's a robust plant and a fibre,
> it's action in the bag and it's a sign.
> It's human time, time that builds up,
> time that is wasted.

But in both of these codes he saw the utopian possibility of a joyful tomorrow challenging the forces of death.

In June 1937 he returned from Mérida to Mexico City and married Elena Garro, who more than twenty years later would be the author of, among many books, a fundamental novel: *Los recuerdos del porvenir* (*Memories of the Future*). She would become, in time, a choreographer, playwright, screenwriter and journalist. In 1939 they had a child, also called Elena and later Helena. They soon separated; they tried living together again in France ten years later but, after multiple difficult periods, they eventually divorced. Octavio Paz describes her as revealed in a beautiful, revealing portrait that Juan Soriano did in 1948:

> [...]
> The pale reflections of her hair
> are autumn over a river.
> A shattered sun in a deserted passageway
> amazing amazed,
> whom is she waiting for, whom is she running from?
> indecisively between terror and desire?
> Did she see filth sprout up from her mirror?

did the serpent coil between her legs?

She wanders through yellow spaces
like a slow feather. Splendour and misfortune.
She stops on the brink of a heartbeat.

[...]

At the moment of marriage, she was about to turn eighteen, and he was twenty-three. They immediately left for Spain because, while in Yucatán, Octavio Paz had received an invitation to attend the Congreso de Intelectuales Antifascistas (Congress of Antifascist Intellectuals) which was about to be celebrated in Valencia.

This trip was fundamental in the poet's development, who again would feel the demands of History that were even more pressing. In the political imagination of writers, a Great Congress is like a Great Crusade: a world meeting of all the writers fighting for the same cause. A Great Congress always revives the warrior imagination, ignites faith and obligates its attendees to polish their weapons. In the 1930's various international writers' congresses took place. They were years of social eruption, utopia and war. One of the most notable was the congress of Valencia, amid the Spanish Civil War. This meeting was known as the Second International Congress of Antifascist Writers for the Defense of Culture. The first had taken place in Paris two years before and, as in this, the declared enemy was fascism. In those years it was not possible to imagine a more real, truer enemy.

These writers defended culture against fascism. Not the existing culture, but a New Culture, that which would be forged in the New Society that they imagined was being built in the Soviet Union.

The proceedings of the 1935 congress reveal that everyone was talking about the New Man. Calling upon good intentions and even better utopias, the organizers of those conferences had certain objectives that were more or less hidden. The main one as to ensure the support of the world's most prestigious intellectuals in favour of the Soviet Union. Very little has been written about the mysterious threads being pulled behind the curtain of those congresses. Nevertheless, Arthur Koestler, in his surprising *Autobiografía*, reveals just who paid for and administered those crusades and took advantage of them as a way of spreading propaganda. It turns out that Koestler, who was a fierce communist militant, worked in Paris as an employee for those offices that covertly raised economic and moral support for the Soviet Union.

The director of this office, Willi Munzenberg, is described by Koestler as the invisible man that made all the arrangements for writers to fight his crusades. And they all became uncritical apostles of Stalin.

Aragon, Éluard, Moussinac, Roland, and Ehrenburg worked for him. Ruth Fischer, the tireless communist militant of that period, would write of this years later:

> It's astonishing to see the success with which communist tendencies were propagated among the social democrats and liberals of that time. Thousands of painters and writers, doctors and lawyers, sang a diluted version of Stalin's directives. All this and more had its roots in the office of Willi Munzenberg.

With the opening of the Soviet archives this hidden, mysterious goal of Munzenberg has been revealed in France as well as Spain. It came with money and direct orders from Moscow. And this especially included the congress of Valencia. This has been confirmed by Munzenberg's biographer, Stephen Koch.

Others, largely sincerely, acted as the face of Munzenberg everywhere: Aragón in France, Bergamín in Spain. Behind them came a mass of writers and artists with their left fists raised; they were unshakeable "true believers." It should not surprise anyone that in the first congress, in Paris in 1935, the case of Victor Serge, who at that moment was being deported to Siberia with the grave accusation of being a "Trotskyist", was strategically and violently minimized by the organizers. It is likewise unsurprising that in the congress in Spain, which Octavio Paz attended, André Gide received a furious condemnation because he had dared to publish a bitter account of what he'd witnessed and lived through in the Soviet Union one year earlier, in 1936. All of this was undermining the young Octavio Paz's faith in the Soviet regime, the causes of communist parties and their methods of getting an uncritical membership.

But apart from the attractive policies that this congress presented, the invitation was also of great importance for Octavio Paz because it was a meeting attended by many of the world's most important writers.

Various artists from the Communist Party of Mexico attended this event, not necessarily as delegates but rather as supportive enthusiasts, especially from the Liga de Escritores y Artistas Revolucionarios (LEAR), of which Octavio Paz was not a member due to his disagreement with their orthodox aesthetic: "socialist realism," "proletarian art," etc.

Only two Mexican poets who were sympathetic toward communism but not officially affiliated with it were invited: Carlos Pellicer and Paz. Among the congress organizers were Rafael Alberti and Pablo Neruda. The former knew Paz personally; the latter had read *Raíz del hombre* (*Root of Man*) and was, as he later stated in his memoir, *Confieso que he vivido* (*I Confess, I Have Lived*), one of the first to appreciate enthusiastically the qualities of the young Mexican poet, who at that time was unknown.

First in Paris and then in Spain, Octavio Paz would meet writers whom he'd never imagined meeting at his age: Neruda, Louis Aragon, César Vallejo, André Malraux, Stephen Spender, Jorge Guillén, Julien Benda, Tristan Tzara, Vicente Huidobro, Miguel Hernández, Luis Cernuda, etc. In Valencia he made friends with the young Spanish poets that edited the magazine *Hora de España* (*Hour of Spain*) and that later would be exiled to Mexico. The experiences of this first contact with Europe were foundational in his life from many points of view.

In Valencia, with an introduction from the Spanish poet and editor Manuel Altolaguirre, he published a new collection of poems entitled *Bajo tu clara sombra y otros poemas sobre España* (*Under Your Clear Shadow and Other Poems on Spain*), 1937. Meanwhile, in Spain he was starting to experience his political doubts that would lead to conflicts with his more "committed" colleagues, causing him to defend a writer's need to remain independent from parties and governments, to think and act on his own.

The case of André Gide and his book, which showed how the Soviet Union – which he had visited in 1936 – was not even remotely the earthly paradise that all the communist militants and even he himself had previously yearned for and defended, is still a testament to the highly intolerant attitudes of the left during that time. In a recent interview about that congress Paz told me the following:

> There was an atmosphere of great pressure and con-
> demnation against Gide. There were various private
> sessions, with the members of Latin American dele-
> gations, in which they discussed Gide's book, his at-
> titude, and the need to condemn him. They proposed
> drafting a letter of condemnation to be signed by all
> the Latin American delegates, and they held a vote to
> get everyone's agreement. On that occasion Carlos Pel-
> licer defended André Gide's right to think differently
> and to express his opinions. In the final vote, which de-
> cided to draft this condemnation of Gide, there were

only two abstentions: Pellicer's and mine. In the end
the condemnation was never written because, in the
afternoon's public session, José Bergamín made such
a violent speech against André Gide that it proved
unnecessary, in the eyes of the different delegates, to
write a new condemnation.

The Spanish writer Ricardo Muñoz Suay wrote me the following in a letter:

I remember that when the writers approached me in
1937 in Valencia, and when I had the chance to talk
with them, I felt drawn to Octavio Paz (who was closer
in age to me) and immediately some friend with the
title of "commissioner" whispered to me that I should
"be cautious with this Mexican who has Trotskyist
whims." In 1937 I was a young man of 19, but an active militant and even a student leader of the Spanish
Communist Party, and I was therefore very sensitive to
the intellectual world of that time. The "treachery of
Gide," in my recollection, has a great impact. It wasn't
one desertion but many others. Gide had a moral pres-
tige as well as an intellectual weight that no one up
to that point had ever cast in doubt [...] On the other
hand, my great friendship with Bergamín and my admiration and certain personal knowledge of Malraux
hardly left me any doubts about the fairness of that
offensive against Gide, in which the admirable Paul Ni-
zan, whom I had known vaguely through Ce Soir, was
also alienated, dead in the stench of betrayal. Many ar-
eas of our society, many of those that in good faith are
"pacifist" combatants still don't want to remove the
blinders from their eyes, but no one can make me for-
get the reasons of these men who, like Gide then and
like Octavio Paz as well as others now, try to reason

face to face with History.

Paz briefly lived through the reality of people in civil war, a reality much removed from the image that his own poems offered of that same war, and that was another, harsher lesson. He returned to Spain with the conviction that yes, certainly, there were causes to fight for in the world, a break from the view of his friends, the poets of the previous generation, that of the Contemporáneos (Contemporaries), especially Xavier Villaurrutia. But the question that was already niggling him before his trip to Spain was intensified with this one: how does one write poetry that is not "pure," but that at the same time is still poetry, not limited or degraded by the aesthetic dogmas of its time? Paz's poetic and editorial work of the following years would form the first responses to that question. Like him, other members of his generation would seek to answer it.

From 1938 to 1941, a magazine was the point of convergence of this new concern, which was also a new sensibility: *Taller* (*Workshop*), which published twelve issues in which the editorial collaboration of Octavio Paz, along with Rafael Solana (the magazine's founder), Efraín Huerta and Alberto Quintero Álvarez was definitive.

One of Paz's texts, "Razón de ser" ("Reason for Being") outlined from the second issue of the publication all of the differences and similarities with the previous generation, that of the *Contemporáneos* (*Contemporaries*) magazine. Dominant among them was the idea of pure poetic rigour, in the manner of Paul Valéry or Juan Ramón Jiménez. In his manifesto, Paz recognized the artistic worth of his predecessors and their creative synthesis of an entire modern age, which Paz and the poets of *Taller* inherited, but he lamented the lack of hope within their artistic revolution. The skepticism of the members of *Taller* is explicit: they were the first generation of writers following the Mexican Revolution. They could not believe that violence might perfectly improve human lives. The new generation did believe that. "This was the postwar generation," Octavio Paz affirmed. "We stand before the next great calamity; they came after it."

Several decades later he would write in his essay "Antevíspera" ("Before Vespers"):

> Although it is impossible for me to summarize in one phrase what separated us from our predecessors, it seems that the great differences lay in the awareness of time that we lived in was more vivid and, if not more lucid, at least deeper and more complete. Time asked us a question that we needed to respond to if we didn't want to lose our face and our soul. We were worried about our situation within History.

In the poetry of that generation, and especially that of Octavio Paz, the answer was taking on an ever more clearly defined configuration, but no less rich and variable: the modern city, with its ruins and promises, was the motif through which appeared a poetry before and inside of History. A new space had been inserted into the poetic landscape of Mexico and Latin America, one that could only be expanded through time.

Some years later, Octavio Paz would become aware that, in other countries, there were already two answers to the questions about a possible happy marriage between poetry and History. One was surrealism, with its powers of rebelliousness and expression. Another was the peculiar solution of T.S. Eliot and Ezra Pound, inserting prosaic, historic elements into poetry and making them poetic.

Both of these would offer important ways out, two experiences with which Paz would enrich the aesthetic vitality of his own work.

No less influential on his poetry and essay writing was the vision of art that he was acquiring. During his trip through Europe he had visited the most important museums of Paris and

Madrid. In France he saw classic as well as avant garde art. Upon his return to Mexico he would take note of the ideological rhetoric of the muralists, whose work he previously had only admired on a daily basis in the frescos of the Escuela Nacional Preparatoria (National Preparatory School) where he had studied. It is not a coincidence that the poet who wanted to base his new poetics on the reality within a city had become initiated into the arts through an urban aesthetic, discovering the artistic and historic richness in the centre of Mexico City.

In 1939 he wrote his first short essay on art: it was called "Isla de Gracia" ("Isle of Grace") and it is about the art of Crete: in 1941 he wrote a more important one on the painter Juan Soriano, and the following year he wrote one on José María Velasco. In these we see the force of expression, the links with the poetic concept developed at that time, and above all else the will (also visible in his literary essays) of turning his gaze into a vision. Because a vision, as he himself says, "is not only what we see. It is a position, an idea, a geometry; a point of view in the dual sense of that term."

In his brief essay on Crete we already see his thirst for new formal and conceptual horizons; in the one he wrote on Juan Soriano we see his poetic proximity to the work and artist that he loves; in the essay on José Maria Velazco he starts to sketch out a philosophy of pictorial forms and also a parallel between the work of Velasco and the landscapes in the poetry of Manuel José Othón. In his last note on art in November 1943, before leaving Mexico for many years, he speaks of the work of Jesús Guerrero Galván and criticizes the classifications of Mexican painting that existed at the time. In this text already he shows a passionate knowledge of Mexican art and the exasperated urge to correct an understanding that he considered to be erroneous.

What is evident in the Paz of that time is the desire, that in his case amounts to a project, of placing himself within a tradition of Spanish language poetry while simultaneously breaking it. He had a desire to discover how - with whatever new costume or metamorphosis suited to his time - the profound, varied destiny of human beings was made manifest, as this was not visible to him in the poetry of his predecessors.

In one of his 1984 *Conversaciones* (*Conversations*) on Mexican television, Paz said the following:

> For us destiny takes on the form of History [...] Never before had the destiny of people, the fact that we are mortal, that we are going to die, that we are capable of loving, that fact that we are born, we work, we do things [...] never had this story been presented in the form of a historic conflict. But this is the case in the twentieth century city. And that was what I found in the poetry of my mentors, the kind I wanted to write.

Beginning with the fifth issue of *Taller,* Octavio Paz was named director of the magazine, and he invited various young Spaniards - whom he had met in Valencia and who were now exiled in Mexico – to participate in it with him: Juan Gil-Albert, Ramón Gaya, Antonio Sánchez Barbudo, Lorenzo Varela, José Herrera Petere. Seven more issues were published, and then the magazine vanished. Paz's polemics with the "committed" writers intensified. Trotsky was assassinated in 1940, and not long before that, the pact between Hitler and Stalin led him to distance himself from his communist friends, some of whom began to defend Hitler with the same fervour. Paz met Victor Serge, Jean Malaquais, and Benjamin Péret, all situated at the left of the left, all dissidents from official communism and Stalinist Russia, and they gave a new meaning to his idea of political criticism.

In the middle of 1942 he published his third volume of poetry, *A la orilla del mundo* (*At the Shore of the World*), where he included some of his old poems with the new ones. Under an epigraph from Quevedo, "Nothing can disappoint me; the world has enchanted me," Paz explored the subtle limits between wakefulness and the kind of sleep of the senses that, in this book, defines the poetic experience.

> We slept on rubble,
> alone among ruins and dreams.
> Your body close to me,
> the dense certainty of your legs,
> your skin and your secret,
> the fragile throbbings of life
> that don't halt the night,
> the brittle stalks of dreams.
> [...]
> You enter even into my blood; in my eyes
> you see yourself and touch yourself; in me you endure,
> turned into calm and word, pure shock,
> detained within yourself.
> You recognize yourself in me and find yourself in me,
> and I recall myself in your sleeping form,
> only a throbbing, a blind flower, a bush,
> land that gets lost among land.

Paz dedicates the last poem of the book to poetry, a character that is constantly present in his work, as are words themselves. In poetry he addresses his beloved. It is powerful, tangible and troubling when he touches it. The mysterious voice of that which is unsayable. Significantly, he says the following:

> You arrive, silent, secret, armed,
> like warriors to a sleeping city,
> an octopus, you burn my tongue with your lips,
> and you awaken the furors, the joys,
> and this endless anxiety
> that inflames all it touches
> and creates in all things

a dark yearning
[...]
You are only a dream
but the world dreams through you
and its silence speaks with your words.

In this poem Paz shows an awareness of his own limits before the excessive force of a vocation, and at the same time he offers a conception of poetry. Paz seeks to profile the nature of his search.

From that point forward, his reflective, sensitive poetry goes on seeking an explanation for its meaning in another genre: essays on the poet's vocation. In April of 1943 he collaborated in the founding of the magazine *El Hijo Pródigo* (*The Prodigal Son*), directed by Octavio G. Barreda. In August of that year he published a new essay that can be seen as a manifesto, "Poesía de soledad y poesía de comunión" ("Poetry of Solitude and Poetry of Communion"). This conception of poetry continued to grow until, many years later, it became *El arco y la lira* (*The Bow and the Lyre*). There he speaks, among other things, of the destiny of the modern poet obligated to write, not outside of society but inside it – which he does not tolerate – and against it. The challenge of the poet is to achieve a rigorous authenticity, "to unite awareness and innocence, experience and expression, the deed and the word that reveals it." A yearning that evokes a man radically alone in the great mass of a city, a man who questions it with his silence.

But it is also a yearning that prefigures the overlap that Paz would later share with surrealism: a vital force that could in part be described as the mysterious union of awareness and innocence, and also the word that becomes deed.

At the end of 1943, Octavio Paz left Mexico and would not come back until ten years later. He received a grant from the Guggenheim Foundation, and two years later he joined the diplomatic service. But before obtaining the grant he earned his living doing various jobs. He sought employment as a gardener or rather the caretaker of the Jardín Parque de Churubusco (Garden Park of Churubusco). Upon not receiving that job, he spent some time in the Bank of Mexico burning paper money that had gone out of circulation.

In between those various temporary jobs that he found in those years he worked for the then prolific Mexican film industry, which was experiencing its Golden Age. The result was the very curious work of Paz, who in 1943 wrote songs for the very popular Mexican singer Jorge Negrete. His friend Jean Malaquais adapted one of Pushkin's plots to make a Mexican film directed by Jaime Salvador and starring Jorge Negrete and María Elena Marqués. The young twenty-nine year old poet who was invited to correct the Spanish dialogues of the Frenchman Jean Malaquais ended up writing several songs .When I retrieved them from an old copy of the film, which at that point was considered lost, and presented them to Octavio Paz, he immediately recognized them as his own. He had not seen them in nearly fifty years. He allowed me to publish them for the first time in *Artes de México* (*Art of Mexico*) in a monograph entitled *Revisión del cine mexicano* (number 10, winter 1991), not without manifesting to me his desire to rewrite them someday in order to include them among his early writings in his complete works. This was something he never managed to do. In one song there are clear echoes of his book *A la orilla del mundo* (*At the Shore of the World*), published one year earlier.

> I look at you with my eyes,
> when I close them I see you
> with locks made of sighs
> in my chest I confine you.
>
> My lips never name you,
> your name is the shaking,

your syllables are the blood
of my heart as it's breaking.

While everything else sleeps at night
I alone can't close my eyes,
I lie awake, feeling you
always at my side

My hands caress you
and my lips, ay, they kiss you
but always, always,
night and day
my thoughts don't cease to miss you.

Yesterday I sang with words
but words break apart
clouds blown off by the wind
today, what sings is my heart.

The movie was called *El rebelde* (*The Rebel*) or *Romance de antaño* (*Romance From Days Gone By*). Although it is dated 1943, it was finished and made its debut in February of the following year. Octavio Paz told me that he did not manage to see its showing as by then he lived in the United States. Maybe if he'd stayed in Mexico the film industry would have more of his contributions. His friends Efraín Huerta and José Revueltas worked a lot for the national film industry, like many other Mexican writers. Paz, however, would be almost unknown during that time to the industry that was experiencing its greatest period.

After leaving his country, Octavio Paz closed one cycle of his life, the first circle of his destiny consumed him; without a doubt, the poet had emerged. But he was already a noted essayist as well, and, in the volume which Enrico Mario Santí edited in 1988, *Primeras letras (1931-1943)*, (*Early Letters*

[1931-1943]), a selection of his prose texts demonstrates that clearly. It contains literary and philosophical essays, poetic prose, reviews of books and explications of real life situations that appear perplexing for the fullness of their aspirations and the power of their prose; a book filled with a headstrong depth of fire. This is the same way that we could define his creative impulse during those years: a flame that is testing itself. It is almost the book of a philosopher who has on his tongue the dazzling weapons of creation.

There is a thinker poet in this young man from the 1930's who eagerly seeks his path, his books, his words, his ideas, his sleeping and waking, his battles and achievements. In the various poems of *Raíz del hombre* (*Root of Man*), in his essays, in his political attitudes there burns with a significance of a profound search the word "tentative." With these he established the foundational territory of his work and his way of being a poet. There he deeply sowed a way of being in the world like a seed that he would find transformed and harvest in the following years. And his trip outside of Mexico would give him the chance to experience a new beginning.

III
Circle of Air
Toward the Unexpected
1944-1958

1. A Flight toward the Orchard of Surprises

Some journeys become an initiation into the diversity of the world, a step into the unknown, an encounter with that which surpasses our mental limits: the discovery that pears can grow from an elm tree. To travel freely can be the equivalent of submitting oneself to the mystery and seduction of another reality. The trip that Octavio Paz began at age twenty-nine contained much of a symbolic exit, a rite of initiation, a new beginning. In a certain way, the poet was born again because his work clearly took another course, but at the same time he resumed his earlier attempts and transformed them into the realizations of a higher creative level. From 1944 to 1959 he published four books of poetry that he considered his own, starting with *Libertad bajo palabra*. These included his emblematic long poem *Piedra del Sol* (*Sunstone*).

His significant contact with surrealism would produce the final form of the dazzling poetic prose of *¿Águila o sol?* (*Eagle or Sun?*). This is also the time in which he would write the two main essays of his work: *El laberinto de la soledad* (*The Labyrinth of Solitude*), his longer poetic formulation, *El arco y la lira* (*The Bow and the Lyre*) as well as the various essays of *Las peras del olmo* (*The Pears of the Elm Tree*). It was thus a period of fruitful achievements. A circle of earth that is transformed into a fruitful cloister, an astonishing garden.

In *Las peras del olmo* (*The Pears of the Elm Tree*) he says that the anecdote of one's life does not explain an artist's artistic fruits.

> The madness of Nerval does not explain the chimeras; the opium of Coleridge does not explain the images of Kubla-Khan [...] What I mean, simply is that the artist transmutes his fate, personal or historic, in a free act. This operation is called creation; its fruit is a painting, a poem, a tragedy. All creation transforms personal or social circumstances into unbelievable works. The human being is an elm tree that always bears incredible pears.

The journey that Octavio Paz set forth on in 1943 began as a geographic one but soon transformed into a journey toward the unexpected garden of his most crucial creation and reflection. His new beginning makes sense but is still surprising. In fifteen years he reinvented himself.

2. First Vision of the Labyrinth

At the end of 1943 he left Mexico for the United States. It was not the first time he had done this. As a child he had lived in Los Angeles during his father's exile. And six years before, in his journey to Spain, he had quickly passed through New York. But on this occasion more than the others he experienced, according to his own words, a "spiritual shake-up." He not only entered slowly into a different country, but being there allowed him to see his own country with new eyes.

He made a long bus journey from Mexico City. He crossed the desert and stopped for some days in Los Angeles. The United States was at war, and this produced a feverish, epic atmosphere that permeated everyone and everything. In factories, shipyards, and workshops, all were working to win the war. The streets were dominated by the vision of men and women in uniform. It was not easy to find food or lodging. Everything was scarce. The strong, singular presence of "the Mexican" particularly attracted his attention. Many years later, in *El laberinto de la soledad* (*The Labyrinth of Solitude*), he would write:

> At the beginning of my life in the United States I resided for some time in Los Angeles, a city with over a million people of Mexican origin. At first glance it is surprising to the traveller – in addition to the purity of the sky and the fidelity of the widespread, ostentatious constructions – the vaguely Mexican atmosphere of the city is impossible to capture with words or concepts. This Mexican-ness – a taste for decorations, dilapidation and splendour, negligence, passion, and reserve – floats in the air. And I say it floats because it neither mixes with nor spills into the other world, the North American one, made with precision and efficiency. It floats, but it does not impose; it balances itself, blown by the wind, sometimes torn apart like a cloud, other times raised up like an ascending rocket. It drags itself, folds itself, expands, contracts, dreams or sleeps in ragged beauty. It floats: it doesn't cease to be, doesn't cease to disappear.

There were groups of distinct young people, the "pachucos," who affirmed their difference through their style of dress. They were above all else of Mexican origin. Paz witnessed the police raids and general persecution of these "pachucos." He saw them as "instinctive rebels" and would discuss them in one part of the first chapter of *El laberinto de la soledad* (*The Labyrinth of Solitude*) entitled "The Pachuco and Other Extremes." Undoubtedly, the experience of that immersion into North American life would permit him, years later in Paris, to write that book.

They were marvellous years: the country believed in
itself and in others. Those years were also very exhil-
arating for me. Not only was there a change in my poetry, but I also came to live with the people of the United States. I viewed them with admiration, envy, love,
and at times horror. I saw myself and Mexico from the
other side. I could discern the stranger that each of us
carries inside ourselves.

From Los Angeles he went to San Francisco and settled at
Berkeley. There, among other experiences, he became famil-
iar with modern English and North American poetry. His ideas
about poetry were transformed. He experienced free verse
with great freedom, and from that point his poems took on a
different character. Thanks to Henríquez Ureña he discovered
that irregular versification existed in medieval Spanish poetry;
therefore, modern poetry could be seen as a return to the oldest traditions of the Spanish language. He studied in depth the
poetry of Walt Whitman, W.B. Yeats, William Blake, Ezra Pound,
Wallace Stevens, William Carlos Williams, e.e. cummings, and
T.S. Eliot. Above all others, Eliot marked Paz in a definitive
way. In his poems the young Paz learned that the past inhab-
its the present, that modernity and tradition can converge in
one work. His poems began to include elements that previously
had been considered incompatible, such as colloquial language
combined with painstaking poetic form. For example, in a poem
entitled "Conscriptos U.S.A." ("Conscripts U.S.A.") he alternates
a dialogue in a bar with more traditionally poetic images. He
significantly places these between parentheses:

[...]
"They locked us in jail.
I mentioned my mother to the corporal.
Immediately the cold-water hose.
We removed our clothes, shivering.
Far too late, they gave us sheets."

(In autumn the river's trees
let their yellow leaves fall
over the water's back.
And the sun, in the current,
is a slow hand caressing
a trembling throat).
"After a month I saw her. First at the movies,
later dancing. We had a few drinks.
We kissed on the corner..."
(The sun, the red rocks of the desert
and an erotic rattle: serpents.
Those cold loves in a bed of lava...)

In a somewhat more elaborate way, in the poem "Seven P.M.,"
the most traditional images are the voice of a ghost that speaks
from within a character who walks through the city. This poetry is also filled with colloquial phrases:

In ordered rows we return
and every night, every night
while we make our way
the brief hell of waiting
and the ghost that weeps into our ears
"No blood yet? Why are you lying?
Look at the birds...
The world still has beaches
and a ship awaits you there, always."

And the legs walk
and a red tide
floods beaches of ash.

"Blood is beautiful
when it springs from certain white necks.
Bathe in this blood:

crime creates gods."

And the man quickens his pace
and checks his watch: it's already time
to catch the streetcar.

Paz's grant from the Guggenheim Foundation lasted approxi-
mately one year. He combined it with a very modest job in the
Mexican consulate and a few collaborations with the press. In
spring of 1945, in San Francisco, there was a celebration of the
international conference whose result would be the foundation of the United Nations. Octavio Paz attended this event as
a correspondent for the magazine *Mañana* (*Tomorrow*). Upon
finishing this work he moved to New York. He had tried to en-
list in the merchant marine but was not accepted. He sought out
Luis Buñuel, whom he had met in Paris during his previous trip
to Spain and France. Buñuel lived in the United States before
settling in Mexico, and Octavio wanted to ask him for employment, but the surrealist filmmaker's situation really was not
much better than his own. One of the many jobs Paz found was
working on the Spanish dubbing of a North American movie.

He was an invited professor at the celebrated summer
school of Middlebury College in Vermont. A wonderful place
where many great writers taught: Jorge Guillén, Eugenio Florit, Pedro Salinas, Luis Cernuda. At that time, on an assignment
from the Argentine magazine *Sur* (*South*), he interviewed
Robert Frost, who lived in a small cabin in a nearby forest. He
received a lesson in joyful thrift, our basic relationship with
nature, and the ways in which this relationship can be transformed into poetry. Everything that the poet lived through in
those years was a lesson in how one's own experience as well
as that of others might be turned into art and writing. Thus,
this journey was the laboratory for his own development as
well as his creative workshop.

In August of that year, the Mexican poet José Juan Tablada

had died in New York. At the request of Columbia University, where the Cuban poet Eugenio Florit taught, he studied Tablada's work and wrote the first modern essay on this author – intended to be read at a public event in his honour – who in Mexico at that time did not enjoy the respect he now holds. Both Alfonso Reyes and Xavier Villaurrutia, for example, viewed him with disdain, and Paz's essay, "Estela para José Juan Tablada" (*A Wake for Juan José Tablada*) led to his reemergence as a valued writer. From that point on, Octavio Paz would disrupt more than once the values of Mexico's literary history and help to shape the face of our modern culture. In order to do this, his work as an editor and a translator was essential.

At the same time, Tablada influenced the poetic work of Paz; he came to form part of his tradition. Also, thanks to Tablada a curiosity was opened in Paz, one which would later become passion, for Asian literature and culture. It was his entrance into another world. One which he would later call, "the other half of our tradition." This was in contrast to those who saw in Tablada an author too literary and pretentious. Paz found in him an invitation to life, adventure and travel.

Significantly, our Mexican poet in New York finishes his homage with these words:

> [Tablada] invites us to keep our eyes open, to know how to abandon our native city and the verse that has been transformed into a bad custom; he invites us to seek new skies and new loves. All of this goes on – he tells us – until death. And, as we already know, to reach ourselves it is necessary to go out and take risks.

Speaking of Tablada, Paz described his own need to go out, take risks, and finally, recognize that he was in the middle of what would be his own transformative journey. All that he experiences is a coded sign that propels his own growth, his ascension toward modernity.

3. When the Work is a Ripening Fruit

In 1944, a friend of his father, Francisco Castillo Nájera, suggested that he join the diplomatic service, something that he would spend the next twenty-three years of his life doing. He was briefly in the consulate in San Francisco and then spent some months in the New York consulate. The Museum of Modern Art became his daily nourishment, as did the seething life of the metropolis.

Thanks to José Gorostiza, who worked in the Secretaría de Relaciones Exteriores (Secretariat of Foreign Relations) and protected him throughout his entire diplomatic career, Paz was sent to the Mexican embassy in Paris. There, occupying a modest position, he began his slow and long diplomatic career. The great playwright Rodolfo Usigli was his work colleague.

Nevertheless, Paris would be for Paz a highly stimulating cultural environment. He arrived with the hope, very common at the time, that postwar Europe would rise up like the Phoenix from its ashes in the form of a new society that would be markedly socialist. He would soon realize just how illusory this idea was. The fiery polemics of that time interested him, especially those of Albert Camus, Jean-Paul Sartre, David Rousset, Raymond Aron, Maurice Merleau-Ponty, and André Breton, who discussed the future of a Europe divided into two large blocks. On that tangle of militant arguments, one young Greek would be the privileged intellectual guide: Kostas, "the sentry, who saw more clearly and more quickly than almost all of us," as Lucien Goldman informed Octavio Paz about this Greek who would soon be among his closest friends of that time. He was the philosopher and historian Kostas Papaioannou (1925-1981), who was at that time exiled in France. There was no one better than him, a clearheaded scholar of Marxism without being a Marxist himself, to be up on the reality of the socialist countries and their concentration camps during those postwar years, but it was also to immerse Paz in ancient Greek and Byzantine art, as well as contemporary music and art. Papaioannou became one of the most important historians and critics of totalitarian systems. And, according to Paz "if any man among those I've known deserves to be called a friend – in the sense that ancient philosophers gave to this word – then that man was Kostas." The intellectual energy (more than influence) that Paz received from Kostas Papaioannou would be fundamental to his journey. With this Greek, whose erudition could only be found between laughter and intelligence, Paz would confirm on a daily basis what he has already glimpsed upon meeting Victor Serge and Jean Malaquais: that political passion can and should be lucid.

El ogro filantrópico (*The Philanthropic Ogre*), a book of critical essays on history and politics that Paz collected in one volume at the start of 1979, was dedicated to this Greek philosopher who was to die in November of 1981. In his memoir, Octavio Paz wrote the long Poem "París: Bactria: Skíros"("Paris: Bactria: Scyros")

> I was thirty years old; I came from America searching
> for the egg of the Phoenix among the ashes of 1946,
> you were twenty, from Greece,
> from the insurrection and the prison,
> we met in a café filled with smoke, voices
> and literature,
> a small bonfire that had lit
> our eagerness to resist the cold and poverty of that
> February
> we met and spoke of Zapata
> and his horse, of the black stone covered
> by a veil, Demeter head of a mare,
> and remembering the lovely sorcerer of Thessaly
> who transformed Lucío into an ass and a philosopher
> waves of your laughter covered the conversations

and the noise of the teaspoons in the cups,
there was a murmur of black and white goats
climbing en masse a land of burnt
hills
[...]
Kostas, among the frozen ashes of Europe
I did not find the egg of the insurrection,
I found, at the foot of the cruel Chimera,
drenched in blood, your laughter of reconciliation.

In Paris he met Henri Michaux, Emil Cioran and Roger Caillois, three profound influences on his work. This was especially true of Caillois, without whose work reflecting on ritual and mythology, on the economy of waste and gift, on the meaning that parties and celebrations have for a group of people, Paz's soon-to-be-written *El laberinto de la soledad* (*The Labyrinth of Solitude*) would be unthinkable.

Thus, Roger Caillois represented an intellectual extreme and a vision of the world that was opposed to surrealism. But in the young Octavio Paz all worthwhile ideas could be joined, and he drank from surrealism as well as the heterodox scientific vision of Caillois with the same alchemical, transformative power. Also in Paris he again saw Benjamin Péret and through him participated in various activities and publications of the surrealist group.

In time he would make friends with André Breton and truly unleash his passionate and permanent – though late – relationship with surrealism. Many years later, in *Corriente alterna* (*Alternating Current*), he would have to recognize the following: "On many occasions I write as if I were sustaining a silent dialogue with Breton: reply, response, coincidence, divergence, homage, all at the same time." In surrealism Paz saw not an aesthetic school or artistic method, but rather a "secret spotlight of poetic passion on our despicable age," a subversion of sensibilities, a radical movement of liberation from art, eroticism, morality, politics, etc. This is to say, above all else, a vital adventure. While incorporating elements of surrealist poetics in his poems, Paz renounced the dogma of the automatic writing and reintroduced the importance of the topic, the theme.

It was precisely that issue, the vital and personalized contemporary history right down to the most quotidian details, that Paz had learned from Eliot and Pound to insert into the poem. In exactly those years, at the end of the decade of the 1940's, the poetic work of Paz would reach its first mature formulation; in 1949 he published his first fundamental poetry book: *Libertad bajo palabra*.

The following year, he published the essay on the nature of Mexican culture that would quickly become a classic: *El laberinto de la soledad* (*The Labyrinth of Solitude*). And one year later, another important book, written in poetic prose under the aura of his new aesthetic formulation: *¿Águila o sol?* (*Eagle or Sun?*) In three years he wrote three important books in his own body of work and in the writing of his tongue and his country.

Libertad bajo palabra is, in part, a revision of his earlier work: rewriting under new demands, but above all else a radical novelty: this book shows itself to be an avant garde work – in the very period of the avant garde's withdrawal and academicism – but a type of critical avant garde that has taken a great leap over the wall of stereotypes. In the poems of *Libertad bajo palabra* there was a new, vital attitude that secretly, and without knowing it, Octavio Paz shared with other Latin American writers of the time. In José Lezama Lima, Enrique Molina, Emilio Adolfo Westphalen, Nicanor Parra, Álvaro Mutis, Gonzalo Rojas and others that at the beginning of the 1950s were along with Paz the initiators of the contemporary poetry of Hispanic America, there is a common poetic future that would later be described in *Los hijos del limo* (*Children of the Mire*) (1974) as a way of living out a language:

It wasn't about trying to invent something, as was the case in 1920, but trying to explore. The territory that attracted these poets was neither outside nor inside. It was that zone where interior and exterior meet: the zone of language. Their concern was not merely aesthetic; for those young people language was, simultaneously and contradictorily, a destiny and a choice. Something we are given and something we make. Something that makes us.

In a central poem of *Libertad bajo palabra,* "Himno entre ruinas" ("Hymn Among Ruins") there appears in his work that new artistic form that Paz would explore more in depth later: simultaneism. With Paz, that procedure is to show two parallel actions at the same time become a new natural form of poetic modernity in the Spanish language, creatively transposing a discovery of Apollinaire and Cendrars in French poetry, and of Pound and Eliot in English poetry. *Libertad bajo palabra* would experience more than seven new editions that each time would transform the book, finally changing it into a revision and in some cases recreation of his poetic work from 1935 through 1957. The first manuscript version of *Libertad bajo palabra* was called *Todavía (Still)* because the author thought of this volume as a kind of test, a confirmation that he was still a poet despite not having published anything since 1942. The book was rejected by an Argentine publishing house that previously had rejected Neruda's book *Residencia en la tierra (Residence on Earth).* Alfonso Reyes helped him to publish it in Mexico at the end of 1949, and the recognition it received was immediate.

The definitive title alludes to a paradoxical conception of freedom as something necessarily conditional. In Greek theatre the destiny that determines us requires the character to have freedom in order for it to be fulfilled. Conversely, since 1935 Paz had written, "freedom is the mask of necessity." In the same way, the freedom of poetry has to flow between precise and often limiting verbal forms in order to exist. Poetry is precisely like human existence: conditional freedom, atheism *bajo palabra*. In fact, this book was thought of as a succession of spaces. Each one demonstrates a facet of the evolution of a spirit, and that spirit is a poet created as a character by Octavio Paz.

With its colloquial language, with its distance from the social poetry evident and its way of situating itself in history, *Libertad bajo palabra* was a break not only from his own earlier poetry but also with what was then being written in Mexico.

He had found his own way of situating history within poetry. There remained the challenge of formulating a more explicit way, in an essay, his concerns about History. That essay was *El laberinto de la soledad* (*The Labyrinth of Solitude*).

Published in 1950, *El laberinto de la soledad* is a response to two basic questions: what does it mean to be Mexican in the twentieth century? And, what does Mexico mean in this period?

The word "solitude" has a predominantly historical meaning in this book: the idea of being alone in time, in history. On the other hand, solitude is a state that Paz considers the destiny of all human beings and all nations. Written in the prose of an essayist who is also a poet, the book is a lucid ritual analysis: the ideas become bedazzlements, visions, revelations. And what he precisely analyses are the most profound myths and rituals of the contemporary Mexican, that is to say, the Mexican that lives in different historical periods simultaneously. For the author, history – as a discipline – is a type of knowledge that is at a halfway point between science and poetry. With *El laberinto de la soledad* Octavio Paz passionately navigates through a haze of identity and offers the coming generations the words to name it.

This book, which reflectively intrudes into the myths of Mexico and Mexicans, became a myth in turn. And not in the sense of a lie (I do not use the word "myth" pejoratively) but rather of a tale that speaks of the origin of a social group and is a tale shared by that group. A tale that with its aesthetic as well as its meaning helps to understand the meaning of life. *El laberinto de la soledad* is one of the principal myths of contemporary Mexican culture, taking into account Lévi-Strauss's affirmation that all deciphering of myth is always a new myth.

The thought of Roger Caillois in *El mito y el hombre* (*Myth and Man*) and *El hombre y lo sagrado* (*Man and the Sacred*) as well as readings from the writer and philosopher Georges Bataille and the anthropologist Marcel Mauss (the ideas of these three thinkers on ritual festival, useful waste, the appearance of the sacred among humans, the hidden dimensions of life) were essential for Octavio Paz in his essay on the Mexican labyrinth. Many of his quotidian observations and discussions of Mexican themes that he had started exploring with his brief articles published in the newspaper *Novedades* (*Novelties*) in 1943 began to have another reach. "It's revealing that our intimacy never surfaces in a natural way, without the catalyst of a fiesta, alcohol or death."

One of the most celebrated chapters of the book, which is a very original and much cited analysis of Mexicanisms, particularly the term "chingada", has its long inspiration in the essays of Borges that are included in "El lenguaje de Buenos Aires" ("The Language of Buenos Aires"). But Octavio Paz tries to interpret these in their ritual sense of the Mexican's constant "search" for a way to transcend loneliness.

In contrast to the treatises of Samuel Ramos on the psychology of the Mexican, Jorge Portilla on "the mess," and Emilio Uranga on the ontology of the Mexican, Paz instead attempted a "space of critical imagination," a literary exploration of hidden, often dangerous beliefs. "My book tried to be an essay of moral criticism: a description of a hidden reality that causes harm."

Published the year after *El laberinto de la soledad* (*The Labyrinth of Solitude*), his book *¿Águila o sol?* (*Eagle or Sun?*) is a series of prose poems, stories, thoughts, and images that constitute a kind of concentration of Paz's poetic attempts up to that point. None of his texts shows Paz's idea of the poet made by language as well as this one does. Each text is an exploration of personal, external and internal worlds and subworlds of Mexico and the world at large. This was literally the "Trabajos del poeta" ("Works of the Poet") writing and living among "Arenas movedizas" ("Restless Sands"), to use the titles of the two sections of a book that contained many of the ingredients needed to be considered part of the surrealist sensibility: an exploration of subterranean worlds, an adventure in the world's unconscious. In fact, one of the poems of this book, "Mariposa de obsidiana" ("Obsidian Butterfly") was Paz's first collaboration in a surrealist publication, when it was included by André Breton in the *Almanaque surréaliste du demi-siècle* (1950).

Thus, in that half of the century, in Paris, Octavio Paz brought together the surrealist effervescence and an exploration of the Mexican underworld. In a later poem, written about an exposition of surrealist art in Mexico, he would mention various surrealist writers and artists as a "convergence of rebellions." In that moment, his own rebellion was also unfolding.

At the 1951 Cannes Film Festival, he met a surrealist filmmaker filled with all things Mexican: Luis Buñuel. This famous filmmaker showed his film *Los olvidados* (*The Forgotten*), with Gabriel Figueroa's photography, taking part in the contest from the sidelines because various atrophied Mexican dignitaries were opposed to him representing their country. Among others, Jaime Torres Bodet alleged that *Los olvidados* gave others a bad image of Mexico. Octavio Paz became a militant promoter of Luis Buñuel and his film. One of his texts, "El Poeta Buñuel," ("The Poet Buñuel") and a poem by Benjamín Péret were printed by them on loose sheets. Ado Kyrou, Bennayou and Paz himself distributed these in the halls and at the events' points of exit. In the end, the film was recognized for all its great worth.

Also in Paris, Paz briefly met Samuel Beckett. It was a circumstantial meeting, strictly for work purposes, that did not result in any friendship. They were completing an editorial assignment for UNESCO. Neither of them knew that both would go on to receive the Nobel Prize for Literature: Beckett very soon, in 1969, and Paz in 1990. The young Mexican poet was preparing and writing the prologue for an educational anthology of poetry from his country intended to be published in French and English by the organization. It was a project of the writer and diplomat Jaime Torres Bodet, then director of UNESCO, and Paz did not have all the freedom he would have liked in the selection process. Beckett was to translate the work into English, though he hardly knew Spanish; he had taken the job out of necessity and, according to what he admitted to Paz, he would need to ask the help of a friend who did know Spanish (most likely Gerald Brennan). The two future Nobel laureates had two or three brief meetings in a café. According to Octavio Paz it was extremely difficult to talk to Beckett, and he could see that he really was not very involved in the translation, except for on three occasions clarifying the meaning of some Baroque poems. There was, according to Octavio Paz, a high level of discomfort for both of them in carrying out this task. And each one was the witness of the other's disengagement and lack of enthusiasm for this project.

At the end of 1951 he reached the end of his first stay in Paris. Those were six years of great creative activity that intensified the change the poet had begun to experience since his time in the United States. The quick vitality that his poetry took on in North America and the patient subtlety that his thought acquired in France gave his passion a new character. The poet and his work, already dazzling, had reached a point of passionate maturity which would be quite worthy of Villaurrutia: "your burgeoning voice, your burning voice, your voice, burned."

4. Return to Mexico from the rising sun

In the year 1952, the diplomat Octavio Paz found himself required to leave Paris and spend the next two years in New Delhi, Tokyo and Geneva. In 1953 he met the painter Bona Tibertelli de Pisis, the wife of his friend André Pieyre de Mandiargues, with whom he would have an intense relationship, among others. After this he would return to Mexico, after nine years of absence, and remain in his country for five years until 1959.

From January through June of 1952 he was in India, where he wrote the poem "Mutra" ("Mathura"), included in *La estación violenta* (*The Violent Season*). There he shows, among other things, his affective relationship with the "spirit of the place." In the poem, a scorching summer overcomes the speaker with the force of an absolute deity:

> Like a too-loving mother
> a terrible mother who strangles,
> like a reserved, solar mother,
> like a single wave the size of the sea,
> she has come in silence and in each one of us
> she takes her seat like a king
> and the days of glass are melted and in each chest
> she raises a throne of thorns and embers
> and her empire is a solemn hiccup, a crushed
> breath of gods and animals with dilated
> eyes
> and mouths filled with hot insects
> pronouncing a single syllable day and night,
> day and night.
> Summer, immense mouth, a vowel made of breath
> and panting!
> [...]

In time, his relationship with India would become, ten years later, a foundational episode in his life. For the time being, in the middle of 1952, less than six months after his arrival, he was transferred from New Delhi to Japan, where he stayed for a little more than six months.

In Tokyo he wrote, also in verse form, the poem "¿No hay sali-da?" ("No Way Out?") included in the same book. Like the poem quoted above, it is highly dramatic. In it his personal drama becomes visible. An intolerable present sucks the meaning out of everything. There's a sense that the best of the past is gone forever and the future does not exist: "This instant has swallowed everything of childhood, and the future is nothing but furniture nailed into place." Throughout the poem the main character's identity escapes. A radical otherness expels him from himself, attracts him, makes him look at himself. The theme of an essential alienation, like a distant echo of Alfonso Reyes's poem "Ifigenia cruel" ("Cruel Iphigenia") is subtly present:

[...]

I am this instant, I suddenly came out of myself,
I have neither name nor face,
the "I" is here, ejected from my feet, watching me,
watching itself watch me watching.

Outside, in the gardens that summer destroyed,
a cigarette shows no mercy to the night.
Am I here? Or, was I here?

Thus, Octavio Paz, violently and somewhat confusedly, experienced his personal reality in the middle of the East's revelation. One might come to think that this otherness and fascination were what saved him in the end.

Little by little, this experience would leave a deep mark on his work. His mid-year journey through Japan prolonged the seduction unleashed by his earlier reading of Juan Tablada, who introduced the *haiku* into the Spanish language. As a result of this attraction to Japanese culture, in 1955 Paz realized, along with his Japanese friend Eikichi Hayashiya, the first translation into a Western language of the book *Sendas de Oku* (*Paths of Oku*) by Matsuo Basho.

Fifteen years later, in a later edition of that book, Octavio Paz tried to describe his fascination with Japan, inscribing it in what he calls the history of the West's Passion for the East. He then distinguishes two recent periods: one that begins in Europe the previous year and ends with the Anglo-American "imagist" poets, another that begins in the United States after the Second World War and still has not finished. The first, according to the translator-poet, is above all else aesthetic and has an influence on the literature of Pound, Yeats, Claudel, Éluard, but the effect is greater in the painting of the impressionists, for example.

> In the second period the tonality has been less aesthetic and more spiritual or moral; I mean we're not just passionate about Japanese aesthetic forms but the philosophical or intellectual currents of which they are an expression – particularly Buddhism. The Japanese aesthetic, better said, the fan of visions and styles that this artistic and poetic tradition offers us, has not ceased to intrigue and seduce us, but our perspective is different from that of previous generations. Although all arts, poetry and music and painting and architecture, have benefited from this new way of drawing close to Japanese culture, I believe that what we're all seeking in it is another lifestyle, another view of this world and as well as the world beyond.

His ties to the East would only grow with time; they would get deeper. The strict, seductive form of the short form *haiku* would occupy a significant space in his poetic work, aiding him in his determination to cling to, in his own words, "the floods of surrealism." Also, he would write various articles on the art and literature of Japan. In his interview with Masao Yamaguchi (included in Hugo J. Verani's *Pasión Crítica* (*Critical Passion*) he declared,

> In the Japanese tradition I found, first, the idea of con-
> centration; second, the idea of the unfinished, of im-
> perfection. To leave something aside, to not finish ev-
> erything [...] With very few elements, Japanese poetry
> says something very intense. This interested me a lot
> precisely because it goes against the Latin tradition, es-
> pecially the Spanish one, taking pleasure in abundance.
> Japanese poetry is a lesson in economy. In India there's a
> lot of exaggeration; they write two million lines where-
> as a Japanese writer would condense meaning into a
> question mark [...] Moreover, Japanese poetry concen-
> trates, in one verse, a great plurality of senses, each one
> filed with meanings; it is filled with meanings. Finally:
> the unfinished. I discovered it in Basho and later in oth-
> er poets and painters. Donald Keene says that the Japa-
> nese aesthetic plays with the idea of the unfinished and
> slightly imperfect. It is like a certificate that time gives
> to human works: the certificate of authenticity [...] The
> poet does not say everything and leaves the reader with
> the possibility of finishing the poem.

Without intending to do so, this reflection on the way in which the artist carries out work in relation to his audience offers a commentary on Octavio Paz's return to Mexico in the 1950's. We can say that the development of this passionate, active, belligerent poet, filled with fundamental experiences and a culture that he had absorbed and lived out in the last decade, above all in his years in Paris, culminates with his return to active public life in Mexico. Seeing the effect that his pres-ence had on the country, one can come to think that for the public figure, for the intellectual that Octavio Paz was in that moment, he needed to re-establish contact with his original cultural medium in order to transform it.

Between the end of 1953 and the middle of 1959 Paz again lived in Mexico City, though he still worked for the diplomatic service. With this return, Paz became one of the most active personalities in Mexico's national culture, introducing new writers from abroad and shedding new light on the painters and writers from Mexico.

> When I came back I met with a group of intellectuals who were still anchored in the dogmas that during that period, thirty years ago, were absolutely sterile: social-ist realism, nationalism, etc. But alongside them there was a group of young people, notably Carlos Fuentes. These immediately became my allies and friends, and together we started an attempt to change Mexico's lit-erary and artistic life [...] We sought to renew, open windows, come to know movements, works, and val-ues that were then unknown (and in some cases pur-posely ignored) in Mexico. There was a hegemony, for example, in that formula of Siqueiros "No path but our path." I initiated a campaign with various battles for new art, especially on behalf of Rufino Tamayo and other painters. And along with all this I wrote *El arco y la lira* (*The Bow and the Lyre*), the final poems of *La estación violenta* (*The Violent Season*), among them "El cántaro roto" ("*The Broken Water-Jar*") and "Piedra de Sol,"("*Sunstone*") and finally some translations.

His impulse was evident in the *Revista Mexicana de Literatura,* directed at that time by Carlos Fuentes and Emmanuel Car-ballo. This magazine published a fundamental essay by Kostas Papaioannou, who is one of the first modern leftist critics of Marxism who was not affiliated with any party.

Along with several other artists, among them the painter Juan Soriano, the playwright José Luis Ibáñez and the writer/

painter Leonora Carrington, in 1955 he founded an experimental theatre group, Poesía en Voz Alta (Poetry Aloud). It
was a true avant garde aesthetic movement led by Juan José
Arreola and created on the initiative of another poet: Jaime
García Terrés. It began as an anthology of poetry meant to be
read on stage. Two sessions: one with Spanish poetry and the
other with Mexican. But on the initiative of Leonora Carrington
and Octavio Paz, who always wanted to take things a little further, it became a theatre company. The group included actors,
directors, writers, and set designers. Why not take things to a
higher level? They tried to recuperate the ritual sense of poetry
on stage, its sacred dimension of communion with an audience.
There were radical ideas of having the audience members wear
costumes or masks. Not all the ideas were viable.

For Poesía en Voz Alta (Poetry Aloud) Octavio Paz wrote
and published his only play, *La hija de Rappaccini* (*Rappaccini's
Daughter*) (1956), a poetic drama in one act, freely based on
a story by Nathaniel Hawthorne. It was staged that same year
under the direction of Héctor Mendoza with stage design and
costumes by Leonora Carrington and music by the brilliant
composer Joaquín Gutiérrez Heras. An ideal garden, a paradise,
contains admirable plants that can turn into venom. Paz returns
to the idea of the beautiful, poisoned woman that appears incessantly in literature from medieval India through Hawthorne.
But he converts it into a praise of the moment, of the fullness of
the instant in the eye of the mercurial tornado of life and death.

1956 also saw the publication of another important book
by Octavio Paz, this one a reflection on poetics, *El arco y la
lira* (*The Bow and the Lyre*). With this he received the Xavier
Villaurrutía prize, the most prestigious literary recognition in
Mexico for a single book. (This is distinct from the National
Prize in Letters (Premio Nacional de Letras) which is given for
a larger body of work, which Octavio Paz would go on to receive twenty years later in 1977.)

El arco y la lira (*The Bow and the Lyre*) is a book that pro-

longs and modifies the questions and answers about the nature of poetry that Octavio Paz formulated nearly fifteen years
earlier in his essay "Poesía de soledad y poesía de comunión."
From the beginning the author did not want his book to be
considered as speculation or theory; he preferred to think of it
as the testimony of an encounter with some poems. According
to Paz, following the image of Heraclitus, the nature of a poetic
human being is simultaneously that of a lyre, whose song situates a poet in the world, and the bow, which shoots the poet
toward something beyond the self.

The three sections which divided the book's first edition
opened with this question: is there an irreducible poetic
speech that is somehow different from all other speech? The
first question led to a study of the characteristics of poetry itself: language, rhythm, verse, prose and image.

The second question launches us toward the world of poetic revelation and inspiration, our journey to "the other shore"
where we might have a poetic experience.

With the third question we see again, somewhat transformed, the author's concern for the relationship between
history and poetry. This is to say, his eternal question about
the ways in which the irreducible act of poetry is inserted into
the world. Once again Paz concludes that poetry should not
merely sing of history, but actually embody it. Once again he
suggests that poetry is a return to the self, to that self's deepest and truest desires. And, he again affirms that solitude
continues to be the dominant note in contemporary poetry.
Erudition and original interpretation of the passionate adventure of contemporary poetry take the lead in this essay. In his
conclusion, the author reopens the questions he raises at the
beginning and casts the existence of any answers into doubt.

In reality, what Octavio Paz leaves open with this book is a
direction taken up in his work as an essayist, which will have
a full and powerful current in all the books that make up his
literary essays, particularly *Los hijos del limo* (*Children of the*

Mire) (1974) and *La otra voz: Poesía y el fin del siglo* (*The Other Voice: Poetry and the End of the Century*) (1990) that can be seen as continuations of *El arco y la lira* (*The Bow and the Lyre*).

In fact, beginning with the second edition (1967) of this book, a text entitled "Los signos en rotación" ("Signs in Rotation") would replace the old epilogue. This is a new poetic manifesto that sustains and explains that modern poetry is not, as has been said, a series of poems about poetry. Instead, the highest form of poetry lies in the negation of poetry, in the critique of language and of poetic experimentation itself. A sign of the times: the poem itself contains the key to its reading, but this should never be a definitive, closed reading.

On the other hand, poetry should not be an invention but a discovery of other people, an encounter with the *otherness* that surrounds us. In this sense poetry is the mysterious, authentic search for a here and now. The theme of poetry and revolution, poetry and society, is revised and again placed inside parentheses, identified by its irrelevance. According to Paz, the poet's mission was previously to offer the purest possible meaning to the words of a tribe; today, the poet's task is to raise a question about that meaning. At the same time, poetry is an attempt to reestablish the union of that which has been separated.

Already in the 1955 poem "El cántaro roto" ("The Broken Water-Jar") casts an indignant gaze on the stark poverty of his country and calls for a new synthesis of that which has been ruptured:

> The interior gaze is released and a world of
> vertigo and flames is born beneath the
> dreamer's forehead:
>
> [...]
>
> Tell me, drought, tell me, burnt land, land of
> broken bones, tell me, dying moon,
> is there no water?

Is there only blood, dust,
footprints of naked feet over thorns,
only rags and insect food and stupor
under the ungodly moon like a golden
tyrant?

[...]

we need to dream backward, to the fountain,
we must row centuries back,
beyond childhood, beyond
the origin, beyond the waters
of baptism,
throw down the walls between man
and man, join again that which was
separated,
life and death are not worlds apart,
we are a single stalk with two
twin flowers,
one must dig up the buried word,
dream toward the inside and also
the outside,
decipher the night's tattoo
meet the noon face to face
and remove its mask
[...]

The publication of this poem in the *Revista Mexicana de Literatura* provoked discontent among the false patriots that did not want to tarnish the institutional lie of a completely modern Mexico. This poem's title was itself iconoclastic: a critique of the national values, a refutation of the idea of the beautiful mestizo nation that gratuitously abounded in the textbooks of the time.

The battles of Octavio Paz and his allies tried to demonstrate that the country still had a long way to go on its path toward truth and modernity. He still believed in this, though his essays at this time were beginning to show indications of what later on would become an open critique of the very idea of modernity. But in that moment the idea of a cosmopolitan, critical and creative modernity was the vision that replaced the socialist dream of his youth.

From that point forward, Paz's activity as a critic and literary essayist was enormous. *Las peras del olmo* (*The Pears of the Elm Tree*) was his first relatively miscellaneous prose volume. It was a selection from fifteen years of literary journalism. In the introduction he apologizes for not including all the themes that interest him or that he feels he should include: the poetry of Xavier Villaurrutía, Alfonso Reyes, Jorge Cuesta, Alí Chumacero. The first part of the text included texts about Mexican poetry: his first essays on Sor Juana de la Cruz, José Juan Tablada, Carlos Pellicer, José Gorostiza, López Velarde, and his introductions to two anthologies, one of contemporary poetry and another of a comprehensive volume of poetry from many time periods. The second part of the book ranges from a text he wrote when young, "Poesía de soledad y poesía de comunión," to his later essays on surrealism and Japanese literature. It also includes his essays on the painting of Rufino Tamayo, Juan Soriano, and Pedro Coronel as well as the work of Spanish writers Machado and Moreno Villa.

From then on we start to see various fundamental ideas that the poet/essayist would develop in time, among these that of modernity in art as a tradition, precisely a tradition made from ruptures. The idea of the decadence of the *avant gardes* is realized through the idea that it is no longer possible to believe in linear, progressive time: the idea of modernity is in crisis, and from this point the notion of the future is dissolved along with the idea of change. Several years ahead of time, Octavio Paz prefigured the problems that would later dwell under the name of "postmodernity."

Octavio Paz's exploration of modernity and its ending have

developed in literature, especially poetry, but also in art and above all else in painting. As a critic of art, Paz opened Mexico up to a new field of modernity that not only informed what he was doing in the world, but also aided in the understanding of the other modern Mexican painters. This included pre-His-panic art which was soon seen with other eyes because his was a gaze that knew how to appreciate the values of "the primitive" as an authentic, marvellous art form – not only as historical testimony or archaeology.

During his return to Mexico in the 50s and after *¿Águila o sol?* (*Eagle or Sun?*), the poetic work of Paz took an ever more reformist, experimental turn. His poetic adventure was paving the way for poets younger than himself who, before finding their own voice, often without realizing it, passed over roads that had first been walked by Paz.

In 1954 he published *Semillas para un himno* (*Seeds for a Hymn*), twenty-two poems of variable form and dimension, where the les-sons of Japanese poetry are already visible in his imagery. A kind of *haiku* serves as the opening for one of the sections:

> Day extends its hand
> Three clouds
> And these few words.

Constant themes in this book include the harrowing aspects of life ("Broken mirrors in which the world sees itself destroyed"), the search for another presence ("Appear / Help me to exist" / Help yourself to exist), and the encounter with the body of another:

> [...]

> You were crying and laughing
> the bed was a peaceful sea

The room was blooming
Trees were being born water was being born
There were bouquets and smiles among the sheets
There were rings at the measure of joy
Unforeseen birds on your breasts
Flashing feathers in your eyes
Your body was like slumbering gold
Like gold and its burning answer when touched by the
light
Like the electric cable that strikes when touched
You laughed and cried
Let us leave our names on the shore
Let us leave our shape
With those closed eyes body inside
Beneath the double arc of your lips
There was no light there was no shadow
Each time further inside
Like two seas kissing each other
Like two nights fumbling to penetrate each other
Each time deeper inside
Embarking on the black sailboat

The following year, 1955, he wrote a set of *haiku*, "Loose Stones," which would later be added to *Semillas para un himno* (*Seeds for a Hymn*). In them he explored, in this extremely brief form, images that recall pre-Hispanic objects and myths. Others reveal a poet astonished by the flashing images of the world. In one entitled "Biografía" ("Biography") we see the strong sensation coming upon the poet that one phase of his life was ending and distancing itself from him. The universal separation of which he constantly speaks in his poetry of that time is also a separation from himself, from what he was and did:

It's not what could be:
It's what was.

And what was is dead.

Seen from the perspective of time, the poems in *Semillas para un himno* (*Seeds for a Hymn*) seem to point toward a much more ambitious fulfillment of the themes and obsessions they inhabit. This realization would be a long poem of synthesis: *Piedra del Sol* (*Sunstone*). It appeared in 1957 as the culmination of a search within his poetry. It is a circular poem that is also a poem about love and the crimes of history. A poem full of mythologies and archetypes. A poem of the encounter with the beloved and with the world in ruins when the sun opens its minds like stones and makes life bloom from them.

Piedra del Sol (*Sunstone*) is a fundamental long poem in the work of Octavio Paz. It is an autobiographical poem but also the biography of a generation. A vision of what remained of his dreams: ruins of the great historic hopes and an affirmation of attempts at and the impetus toward love, as what remains is life itself. An *eros* that is total and that in this moment is the dominant sign of his poetics:

[...]

I navigate your waist like a river,
I explore your body like a forest,
like a mountain path
that ends in a sharp abyss,
I follow your cutting thoughts
and the exit of your white forehead
my tumbling shadow is ripped,
I pick up my fragments one by one
and proceed without a body, fumbling in the dark,
[...]
I want to go on, continue beyond, and I can't;
the moment tumbled into another, then another,
I had dreams of a stone that does not dream

and at the end of years like stones
I heard my imprisoned blood sing,
[...]

In 1958 *La estación violenta* (*The Violent Season*) appeared, including the previous poem, and in 1960 this whole book would be included in the new edition of *Libertad bajo palabra*, retrospectively closing a cycle of Paz's life and work.

In 1959 he formalized his divorce from Elena Garro. In all those years there was very little time in which they truly lived together as a loving couple. According to the Argentine writer José Bianco, who was a friend to both, each of them led their own frenzied loved life; Octavio's is evident in the radiant erotic poems of *Piedra del Sol* (*Sunstone*). There were efforts to reconcile and start again, especially when Paz had finished his diplomatic work in Paris. But every effort failed. In the middle of 1959, Paz again would leave Mexico for Paris. But his presence, his footprint on his own country was already clear, and even from India, where he would reside starting in 1962 as ambassador, his connections to the cultural life of Mexico would be much tighter than during his previous departures. In fifteen years he had lived with enormous intensity a long, transformative journey; he had absorbed everything in order to change it into a surprising poetic work, and in the cultural life of Mexico he was already leaving a mark, an irreplaceable presence.

IV.
Circle of Fire
The Fleeting Paradise: 1959-1970

1. New Old Worlds: an Indian Parentheses

When Octavio Paz was forty-four, his book of poems, *La estación violenta* (*The Violent Season*) began to circulate. With this expression the poet was referring, among other things, to the end of his youth. He felt the need to close one period and begin another. Thus, in the following year (1959), this forty-five year-old poet began a relatively different life. He would spend the next decade in France and India. He would be in Paris for the first three years and New Delhi after that, where his vital, creative search would find an oasis of fullness.

Nevertheless, after this period of luminous calm in the East that would last until 1968, destiny appeared to be offering him a new, very agitated season. The autumn of his life was going to be more violent than his summer, and his new age ever more dynamic.

The poems that he wrote between 1958 and 1961 were published the following year in the book *Salamandra* (*Salamander*), and they intensely reveal a poetry that, as the author had already noted, lives and grows; it creates and recreates itself in the critical reflection of itself. In the same volume we see equally intense short poems about erotic encounters, images presented with the tone of Japanese poetry. There are also blooms of surrealism, like in this poem that occurs in Paris and involuntarily recalls the painter Magritte:

He walked along the crowd

along Sebastó Boulevard,
absorbed in his own thoughts.
The red light stopped him
He looked up:
          above
the grey rooftops, silver
among the dreary birds,
a fish was flying.
The traffic light turned green.
As he crossed the street he asked himself
what he was thinking about.

In another poem which also takes place in Paris, following an encounter with André Breton and Benjamin Péret, the invisible is made present and the city becomes a woman, a presence:

At ten p.m. in the Café de Inglaterra
just us three
      there was no one else
Outside you could hear autumn's humid footsteps
footsteps of a blind giant
footsteps of the forest reaching the city
[...]
Everything is a door
the light pressure of a thought is enough
Something is preparing itself
one of us declared
[...]
City or Woman Presence
fan that reveals and hides life
beautiful like the mutiny of the poor
your forehead raves but from your eyes I drink sanity
your armpits are night but your breasts day
your words are stone but your tongue is rain

your back is the noon of the sea
your laughter is the sun rising in the outskirts
your loosened hair is a storm over dawn's
     terraces
your womb is the sea's breath and the day's throbbing
your name is torrent and your name is meadow
your name is high tide
you share all the water's names
But your sex is unnameable
[...]

Upon his return to the Paris which he knew so well and recognized as his own, he perceived the cultural changes that were occurring at the end of the 50s and the beginning of the 60s. Already from Mexico he had been writing about the signs of a new avant garde that was appearing in the 50s. The decade of the 60s was starting and many of his doubts about those years would appear in the brief articles and essays brought together under the title *Puertas al campo* (*Doors to the Country*) (1966), but especially in *Corriente alterna* (*Alternating Current*) (1967), which, among his books of that period, was the one most clearly linked to the time when it was written. It includes texts published in different magazines from 1959 through 1965, grouped in three sections. The first has to do with art and literature. There appears the premonition of what would be the artistic atmosphere of the sixties: "Another time is dawning: another art." The second edition is dominated by those themes that can now be seen as the footprints of the period: the "artificial paradise" of drugs and literature, freedom, atheism and cults in the West, Buddhism in the East. The third part deals with politics: for many years the poet would contemplate the difference between revolution, riot and rebellion.

The themes that soon would be the cultural air we all breathed in the sixties could be found in those articles by Paz, sometimes earlier than in other texts of our language. All the

books of essays that he wrote in that decade give a testimony
to his passions and obsessions of the time.

In Paris he began to create for himself a somewhat rarefied
cultural atmosphere dominated by the idea that all is language: a system of signs. In everything there is nevertheless a
hidden structure that it is necessary to untangle: this theoreti-
cal and interpretive effervescence would come to be known as
"structuralism." The lexicon of literary studies would become
saturated by the word "sign" and other related terms, and under that emblem of the world as language Octavio Paz would
give his books titles that reflected the emblems of his time:
Los signos en rotación (*Signs in Rotation*) (1965), *Conjunciones
y disyunciones* (*Conjunctions and Disjunctions*) (1969) "about
the relations of affinity and opposition," union and separation
of signs; the sign that is body and the sign that is not body,
as he would explain in the book. Later, *El signo del garabato* (*The Sign of the Scrawl*), with texts written between 1967
and 1972; *Teatro de signos/Transparencias* (*Theatre of Signs/
Transparencies*) (1974), a grouping of texts put together by Ju-
lián Ríos, and *El mono gramático* (*The Grammarian Monkey*),
a long prose poem that closes his Eastern cycle. Meanwhile,
in the middle of the decade he would complete a book on one
of the fathers of French structuralism: *Claude Lévi-Strauss o el
nuevo festín de Esopo* (*Claude Lévi-Strauss or Aesop's New Banquet*), where he would define the human being as an emissary
of signs and as a sign among signs.

Paradoxically, his reading of structuralism was that of a man
of letters of a fuller horizon than that of a semiologist, and for
that reason he would later remain relatively on the margins of
the great structuralist trend, whose diffusion and fortune lay
more in the hands of the technicians of this discipline. The so-
called "sciences of language" were transformed into a technology for interpreting the world. The humanist impulse of Paz
came from other sources and went in another direction, but
like so many things that he witnessed, he absorbed it all and

managed to convert it into a very personal work.

For the Secretarial of Foreign Relations of Mexico, naming Paz ambassador to India was not so much a distinction as a gesture of disrespect. "You must understand that I cannot offer you anything better," he said. But that seemed like a negative move for someone with more than twenty years of life as a diplomat. Paz managed to transform this into one of the best moments of his life: the intense discovery of an alternative world, the chance to see the world from another angle, and also the chance to have more time for writing. In India he would complete, as we can see in his bibliography, many essays. In the majority of these there is a concern with examining the insertion of art in its time, almost always against the current or, as the title of one of his books puts it, toward an alternative current.

The movement in which Paz situates himself is clearly a movement of rupture. Thus, the four poets about whom he wrote long essays during this decade – Rubén Darío, Ramón López Velarde, Fernando Pessoa and Luis Cernuda – are writers that went against the immediate tradition. They are also creators of a new tradition to which Paz himself belongs: the tradition of rupture. "It is the tradition of our modern poetry [...] a movement initiated at the end of the past century by the first Hispanic modernists that still has not ended," as he expresses in the prologue to the book that contains these essays: *Cuadrivio* (*Quadrivium*) (1965). One of them, that which explores the poetic world of Fernando Pessoa, is dated originally in Paris, 1961; the other three are dated in New Delhi, 1964.

That year, after the appearance of *Salamandra* (*Salamander*), Octavio Paz received the Gran Premio Internacional de Poesía (Grand International Poetry Prize) given by the Casa Internacional de la Poesía (International House of Poetry) in Brussels, Belgium. This was the first of many international distinctions that Paz would receive from that moment.

Also, in that same year (1964) Paz married Marie José Tramini. He had met her two years before, upon arriving to India. She was married to a French diplomat. But his meeting with Marie-Jo was absolutely magnetic, and already in 1964, a lovers' elopement took place. They met again by chance in Paris and, as Octavio Paz, "Our bodies spoke to each other; they joined and fled. And we went with them." And for the following thirty-four years, they were not separated for even one day. She returned to India to become the wife of the Mexican Ambassador.

> Aside from being born, this is the most important thing that has happened to me – Paz affirms. We got married under a large tree. A very lush neem. It was filled with squirrels, and above it, in the highest branches, there were some eaglets and also some ravens [...] In the winter afternoons that garden was lit up by an even light, a light outside of time. A light that I would call impartial, reflective. I remember saying to Marie-Jo, "It will be hard for us to forget the lessons of this garden." Lessons of friendship, of fraternity with plants and animals. We are all part of the same whole [...] For the Indians nature is still a mother that can be benevolent or terrible. Also, there are not clear boundaries between the animal world and the human one [...] India taught Marie-Jo and me about the existence of a civilization distinct from our own. And we learned not only to respect it, but also to love it.

His interest in the cultures of India would reappear in several essays, generally as a counterpoint to Western culture. This occurs in *Conjunciones y disyunciones* (*Conjunctions and Disjunctions*) (1968) and in *"Apariencia desnuda: la obra de Marcel Duchamp"* (*Naked Presence: the Work of Marcel Duchamp*) (1973). But it is above all in poetry where his experiences of

India and love would leave their most profound footprints.

The poems of *Ladera este* (*East Slope*) written between 1962 and 1968, show a radical transformation in the poetics of Paz understood as erotism. The poet who traverses the Eastern slope of life re-encounters the reality of this world through the beloved person. This encounter becomes a reconciliation with matter and its questions. The poetic procedures acquire a new calm in which the whirlwind of innovation works from within, very much in the background, transforming everything.

This is evident in the poem "Viento entero" ("Wind from All Compass Points"), where the intensity and fullness of the instant makes all times into a portion of eternity, of paradise. The presence of the beloved, the body around her and the condition of that paradise where even the poet's childhood acquires another light, another transparency. "Each caress lasts for a century." And in a delicate refrain that recurs in each scene, the poet affirms that the present is perpetual:

Two or three birds
invent a garden
            You read and eat a peach
over a red quilt
            naked
like wine in a glass pitcher
[...]
            The present is perpetual
The sun has gone to sleep between your breasts
The red quilt is black and it throbs
Neither a star nor a jewel
            a fruit
you call yourself a date
            Datia
salt castle if you will
            scarlet stain
over a hardened stone

Galleries terraces stairs
abandoned wedding halls
of the scorpion
            Echoes repetitions
erotic clockwork
      the wrong time
                  You walk
the dismal courtyards beneath ungodly snow
a cloak of needles over your unharmed shoulders
If fire is water
            You are a translucent drop
the real young woman
            the world's transparency

While in the earlier periods of his work, Paz's poetry is erotism
in which poetry means stepping out toward the other, encoun-
tering the other, after India there is a new wisdom – which is
also expressed clearly in *El mono gramático* (*The Grammarian
Monkey*) thanks to which the poet, following a path toward a
certain place, suddenly realizes that the journey is the desti-
nation. When asked about this topic specifically, Octavio Paz
recognized that

Suddenly in India, through my personal experiences,
I find a rich cloth of sensations, ideas and experiences. Erotism, for example, neither separates me from
nor draws me close to the sacred. This experience
is very difficult for a Westerner. Erotism is sexuality
transformed by imagination. Love in this erotic imagination becomes a person's choice. And that is what I
discovered in India and what probably changed my poetry. On the one hand it gave more reality, more density to my words. They became fuller. They also became
more lucid. This was, in a certain sense, a rediscovery
of the reality of this world through the beloved person.

And another very important thing is what allows us to realize that the world, though real, is not solid. It is changing incessantly. This tree that I am seeing now is not always the same tree. It is always at the point of falling, of dissolving and being reborn in another tree that is identical to the one that was there one second earlier, but it is not the same. And this also happens with me and with the people around me. Suddenly the universe transformed me not only into a presence, but also a question. This is what I tried to say in my poems; I don't know if I said it, but it was what I tried to say.

Life is the instantaneous fullness of a translation. Thus, in the poem "Pasaje" ("Passage"), again speaking of the beloved, he says,

> More than air
> > More than water
> > more than lips
> > > gentle gentle
> > Your body is the footprint of your body.

His poem "Felicidad en Herat" ("Happiness in Herat") meaningfully dedicated to Carlos Pellicer, a Christian poet who appreciates the fullness of nature, begins and ends thus:

> I came here
> > as I write these lines,
> > without a fixed idea;
> > a blue and green mosque
> > six shattered minarets
> > two or three tombs,
> > memories of a holy poet
> > the names of Timur and his lineage
> > [...]

I saw a blue sky and all shades of blue
from white to green
the whole fan of the poplars
and above the pine tree, more air than a bird,
the black and white blackbird.
I saw the world resting on itself.
I saw the appearances.
And I gave that half hour a name:
Perfection of the Finite.

2. Space as Time and Poem

In 1967, a special edition, appropriate in its experimental
form, was printed of the original edition of the poem "Blanco"
("White"). A single sheet is stretched and, when unfolded, in a
certain sense it produces text by transforming the space itself
into a text. The idea is that reading it should become a ritual, a
journey with various possibilities for which direction to take.
Three parallel columns with different types of printing offer at
least six combinations or possibilities for reading. Paz sought
to emphasize the presence of space in the poem.

One year earlier in his *Topoemas* (*Topoems*) he had exper-
imented with following the road of Apollinaire's calligrams
and Tablada's concrete poetry. The vast majority of poems included in *Ladera este* (*East Slope*) (1969) which also includes
"Blanco" ("White") in its linear version – the poetic procedures acquire an immense calm and a special control of verbal
flow. There are also short poems filled with humour and irony.
In 1969 spatial experimentation and the art of combinations
arrive at a culminating point in his work, when he publish-
es, in collaboration with the painter Vicente Rojo, his *Discos
visuales* (*Visual Discs*). This is followed by the unique experience of *El mono gramático* (*The Grammarian Monkey*), written
in 1970 but not published until 1972 in French and 1974 in
Spanish, but formed during his six years in India. In addition

to the beauty of prose filled with the intensities in which it was written, the book is again a synthesis of Paz's efforts over a period of several years. In this book, to write is simply to go. And one goes along the road of Galta, getting lost while advancing forward, leaving us, little by little, in our own hands: defenceless before ourselves. Several times we find the way and then get lost again. Are we ourselves the road, or is it everything that might distract us? The book advances like a spiral. Poetry is finally a convergence of all points, and it is an act that is simultaneously a body. A poem is written to be read: both actions coincide, and in so doing both are reconciled and freed.

Dated in September 1966, in Delhi, there appeared that same year his prologue to the anthology of Mexican modern poetry that is now classic in its genre: *Poesía en movimiento. México, 1915-1966* (*Poetry in Motion. Mexico, 1915-1966*). This is significant for his personal trajectory because no less important than his role as a creator and witness of his time is that as an editor and promoter of poetry. Many young poets have relied on his reading, opinion, and support. Among these are three Mexican poets, Alí Chumacero, Homero Aridjis and José Emilio Pacheco. Octavio Paz edited that volume in which he proposed a "rescue of the instants in which poetry, in addition to being a frank artistic expression, is a search, a mutation, and not merely an acceptance of one's inheritance." His letters with Arnaldo Orfila on the edition of this anthology demonstrate the rigorous criteria that guided Paz in his selection of poets. There was a clear aesthetic criterion of searching that rejected the kinds of compromises with the literary standards that Torres Bodet had set out in that UNESCO anthology and with which he never felt satisfied. *Poesía en movimiento* (*Poetry in Motion*) is something more than an anthology: it is a true manifesto of poetics in various voices. Finally, Paz wrote to his editor, "Here no compromise is possible. Even if we accept the basic idea of decorum, within it we must strictly apply the other criteria: adventure, exploration, experiment [...] I believe we should reject fixed forms to whatever degree possible."

The following year, in 1967, Paz was accepted as a member of El Colegio Nacional. His "Inaugural Lesson" was to be an essay on Claude Lévi-Strauss. His cultural presence continued growing in his country despite the great physical distance. His season in India is undoubtedly one of his most productive and happy. Nevertheless, that parentheses was closed in October of 1968. Faced with the massacre of students in the Plaza de las Tres Culturas in Tlatelolco, Octavio Paz resigned from the diplomatic service of his government. This closed one period of his life and initiated another, which was more agitated by the social conditions in which he found himself. Paz felt obligated to abandon the "east slope" of his itinerary. It ultimately amounted to an expulsion from paradise.

Many years later, in 1995, Paz would publish a passionate book that is like a return to this paradise that had been taken from him: *Vislumbres de la India* (*Glimpses of India*). Paz defined it as a long footnote to what he considered his real diaries of India: *Ladera este* (*East Slope*) and *El mono gramático* (*The Grammarian Monkey*). It is an essay that gives his poems an intellectual context rather than a vital one. And he concludes, "This book is not for the specialists: it is not a child of knowledge, but love." Nevertheless, the whole first part of the book is a fascinated memoir of his stay in India, including the hasty encounter with Marie José. His description of his arrival at Bombay is dazzling. And the rest of the book is a *sui generis* cultural essay. "This is an attempt to respond to the question that India asks of all who visit." But the book that begins as an enchanted memoir ends in the same way. As a kind of ritual, right after his resignation, Marie-Jo and Octavio traveled to Elephanta Island, where both, before meeting each other, had received their first aesthetic impression of India. There again they lived with that discovery of a landscape that was astonishing for its beauty, and in the half-light of a cave,

the statues, images of beings that are of this world
and of another that we can only glimpse [...] It revived
what we had felt years before. But illuminated by another, more serious light: we knew we were seeing all
of it for the last time. It was like moving away from
ourselves. Time was opening the doors. What awaited
us?

That night Paz wrote a poem in the form of a prayer to the images of Shiva and Parvati.

                    the woman who is my wife
         and I
              we ask for nothing
              nothing from the other world
                                   only
         light over the sea
         barefoot light over the sea and earth as they sleep.

V.
Circle of Water
The New Violent Season
1971-1990

1. Action and History

Octavio Paz's renunciation and his declarations to the international press infuriated his government. The official press attacked him. Many more times in the following years he would be the subject of public controversy for expressing his opinions and also for his political positions. He would never return to the diplomatic service. One poem, "México: olimpiada de 1968" ("Mexico: 1968 Olympics"), written in anger over the news of the massacre, was included as an "intermittence of the West" in *Ladera este* (*East Slope*). Another poem of "intermittence," entitled "Canción mexicana" ("Mexican Song") defines his state of mind and the different way of his political action:

My grandfather, over his coffee,
spoke to me of Juárez and Porfirio,
the Zouaves and the Silver Band,
And the tablecloth smelled of gunpowder.

My father, over his drink,
spoke to me of Zapata and Villa,
Soto y Gama and the Flores Magón brothers.
And the tablecloth smelled of gunpowder.

I remain silent.
Of whom could I speak?

His tablecloths did not smell of gunpowder but of burning ink, but his cultural battles would shake the cultural reality of his country as much or more than those of his ancestors. The poet then returns to a new violent season, a time of burning reason, and he writes a lucid and combative essay on Mexico where he makes open reference to the student movement and the killing at Tlatelolco, to the lack of democracy in the country and the alternative politics of the moment, including a critique of the illusions of development. First he diffuses this as a lecture from the University of Texas. Later it would appear as a book in Mexico under the title *Posdata* (*Postscript*) (1970) because he considered it to be an extension of *El laberinto de la soledad* (*The Labyrinth of Solitude*). It is a critique of the government but, more profoundly, a critique and decoding of the history of Mexico, with all its errors and recent horrors; a "Crítica de la pirámide" ("Critique of the Pyramid") and of the idols within ourselves.

After giving lectures at various universities in England and the United States, he returned to his country. His previous return in 1953 had been marked by his need to bring Mexican culture up to date with the times. At the start of the 1970s, his political interests especially stood out. In 1989 he explained it thus:

> in the decade of the 1950s, when I returned, the most important thing was to express what Mexico is. When I returned in the 1970s the fundamental thing was to reflect on Mexico in order to change it. And that is what we are still living through.

The need for cultural action "to open spaces for the critical imagination" seems to be the new sign of his relationship with his country. The ideas of Octavio Paz have also had a noticeable echo in Latin America and, on certain occasions, they have given rise to great polemics. Ten years after *Posdata*

(*Postscript*) he published a thick volume of historical and political criticism, *El ogro filantrópico* (*The Philanthropic Ogre*).
The title designates the principle characteristics of the Mexican state. The first section of the book, "The Present and its
pasts," contains essays on Mexico that stem from his analysis
in *El laberinto de la soledad* (*The Labyrinth of Solitude*) and
Posdata (*Postscript*). The second involves a history of Mexico,
and the third deals with totalitarianism and erotism. Finally,
the volume unites various essays on intellectuals and power:
dissidence, according to Paz, is the nobility and honor of our
time.

Tiempo nublado (*Cloudy Weather*) (1983) brings together
essays on international politics, the United States' crisis of im-
perial democracy and the Russian crisis of bureaucracy. He especially focuses on the nature of the relationship between the
United States and Latin America. In all his political essays, Paz
affirms the need for the modern intellectual to be critical and
independent from parties and the sciences of truth. He defines
his work as a political analyst as having the inquisitive passion
of a writer, a poet who outside of poetry also provides a testimony of his time. A great part of his literary and political articles were first published in the magazines he edited in Mexico
from the start of the 1970s: *Plural* (from 1971 through 1976)
and *Vuelta* (*Return*) (from 1976 to his death in 1998). These
two magazines will be seen many times at the centre of the
political and cultural debates in which Paz would participate
in his final two decades, the years of his new violent season.
But his literary and philosophical activities would soak into
this deeply, leading him to work with the same experimental
rigor that is present in his poetic anthology of previous years.
Through Paz, the world's foremost writers would find an open
door in Mexico.

In all Latin America those two decades are undoubtedly
stained by freedom-seeking ghosts, very similar in some re-
spects to those of the 1930s. The cultural atmosphere where

Paz played his role of revealing these ghosts in an environment of accelerating authoritarianism was sometimes hostile
to him. His political pen, his critical words, continued to hit
many nerves.

The clearest demonstration of this was when a paper figure of Octavio Paz was burned in effigy in 1984, placed in a
tree by an agitated crowd. It was an act of propaganda that
sought to uncritically favor the militant left-wing Sandinista
movement that was governing Nicaragua at the time. It was
a government that demonstrated a desire to install a bureau-
cratic-military dictatorship similar to that of Havana. For its
part the United States, always interventionist, was support-
ing a rival guerrilla movement, the Contras, formed from a
variety of factions.

Upon receiving the Peace Prize of the German Book Trade,
Octavio Paz made a speech in which he praised the anti-in-
terventionist foreign policy of Mexico in the Contadora Group.
This tended, according to Paz,

> to create conditions in which foreign interventions
> might cease and the contenders might drop their
> arms and initiate peace negotiations. This is the first,
> most difficult step. It is also imperative to understand
> that any other solution – the military victory of one
> group over another – would only be the explosive seed
> of a new, even more terrible conflict. Finally, I want to
> show that the pacification of the region will not be ef-
> fectively achieved until it is possible for the people of
> Nicaragua to express their opinion through truly free
> elections in which all parties participate.

That declaration in favor of democracy and against the Sandinista regime would not be tolerated or even listened to at that
time. It was massively condemned in the newspapers by edi-
tors who were enthusiastic about the utopian socialism they

believed was coming to fruition in Nicaragua. The communist press agency in Germany affirmed that Paz had come out against the Sandinistas to the extent of seeking North American intervention. This defamation was repeated by many commentators in Mexico without seeking verification and clearly used by pro-Sandinista organizations to mobilize a great degree of support for the military regime. Hundreds of intellectuals signed open letters against him. There were speeches in the Legislative Chamber. A boycott of his poetry at festivals. This was the most shameful period in the history of Mexican journalists uncritical of the left; progressive intellectuals and those masses who are easily organized by parties and partisans. In the long run there were free elections in Nicaragua and, against their expectations, the militant regime that won with armed struggle was defeated at the polls. Octavio Paz, as on many other occasions, knew to look deeper and further toward the future. But this was not without paying a price in the form of public shaming.

For example, his critique of Russian totalitarianism – present in his writings since the 1950's and in his thinking since the 1940's, when he began his friendship with Kostas Papaioannou– is seen during many years by the intellectual class or by journalists as "reactionary thought" and "complicity with imperialism." Later, when Russian totalitarianism collapsed and brought its ideologies down with it, they would come to see it as a "premonition." But they were incapable of accepting that all along it had simply been an analysis of reality.

In January 1990, seeing the overwhelming, accelerating crisis of the Soviet regime, Paz offered a historical-political analysis and published *Pequeña crónica de grandes días* (*A Small Chronicle of Grand Days*) (1990). In the introduction he summarizes the major events that substantially affected his life and the process by which he became an active and polemical political analyst:

I was born in 1914. I opened my eyes to a world ruled
by ideas of violence, and I started to think in political
terms as I watched the tumult convulsing Spain in war,
as I saw Hitler's rise to power, the decline of the European democracies, Cardenas, Roosevelt and the New
Deal, Manchuria and the Sino-Japanese War, Gandhi,
the Moscow trials and the apotheosis of Stalin, who
was adored by countless European and Latin American
intellectuals. I started learning about ideas that little
by little became muddled; I then became a theatre of
many internal debates that were quick to become public discussions. I am not proud of these disputes, but I
don't regret them either.

Before the coarse Hegelian idea, which is present in Marxism
and its derivations, that sees history as an absolute which
progresses inevitably toward socialism for all people, and
that critics of this idea are "reactionaries" who oppose human
progress, Paz concludes the introduction to his *Pequeña crónica de grandes días*, affirming

Every historic event, by its very nature, is an enigma.
History is always wrapped in accidents, misfortunes
and catastrophes. Before history the critical spirit
must not weaken [...] History is not an absolute; it occurs through a process that affirms and negates itself
without end. History is time; nothing within it is dura-
ble and permanent.

There were those who wanted to see in Paz's work two distinct mentalities, one in poetry and another in politics. They
did not realize that the restless, unsettling lucidity of the critical thinker was only possible because he lived in the world,
viewed it and thought about it as a poet. With self-reflective
doubt, considering each historic event as a new enigma that

would need to be considered without prior judgment – that is to say, without prejudice.

2. Memory and Melancholy

Paz's determination to maintain doubt in contrast to the political certainty of others suggests a movement toward doubt in the poet's own vital situation in the world and a rereading of his own story. During his return to Mexico his poetry would acquire a tone that openly drew on memory; evoking shadows, it reveals his past. While his political writings were his daytime activity, a study of and confrontation with the philanthropic ogre, his poetry was a return to himself, a nocturnal reflection. His impulse toward poetic creation in the 1970s is a nocturnal force, and the poems themselves are nocturnal.

As a prolongation of his Asian period, in 1971 he had published a collaborative poem, written in a Paris hotel after he had left India. It was written in the Japanese style of a *renga*, and it included the participation of French writer Jacques Roubaud, Italian writer Edoardo Sanguineti and English writer Charles Tomlinson. With the latter he would later attempt a poem in two voices entitled *Hijos del aire* (*Children of the Air*) (1979).

The book *Vuelta* (*Return*) brings together poetry written between 1969 and 1975. These are the poems of his homecoming, not only returning from the geographic East but also the poetic direction that he poet had been following. Memory reveals an "immemorial landscape." A time beyond time in which everything is the present. The centre of that impulse is not the exploration of memory, but that of the poetry that creates and recreates subverted worlds as it is made, spoken and read.

Poetry is not a chronicle of the past but an act nourished by it in the present. In it there appear the friends and city of the 1930s; they appear with the tranquil breath of all his "Errant gardens." Octavio Paz always closes and opens periods of writing with his long poems, which act as hinges. In each of these poems he reveals a renewed poetics. The long poem of this period is "Pasado en claro," ("A Draft of Shadows") written in 1974 and published the following year. In this, the poet invokes and allows himself to be possessed by an eruption of the past. A new grammatical structure of the world takes its form and the poet recognizes, among all the references to the past lives of others, his own references. The old, crumbling mansion of his childhood returns, filled with ghosts.

"When I speak of the house, cracks spread through my words," says Paz. "In my house the dead matter more than the living." "But as the house collapsed, I grew. I was (I am) grass, weeds amid anonymous debris." Upon finishing the poem, action, poem and poet are made and unmade: they are confused with one another. "Steps inside of me, ears with eyes, the murmuring is mental; I am my steps, I hear the voices that I think, the voices that think me as I think them. I am the shadow cast by my words." A new publication of all his poetry written between 1935 and 1975, entitled *Poemas* (*Poems*), brought all his work together in 1976.

A re-edition, but also a rewriting. On one occasion, after learning that in that book he had written different versions of his poems, I asked him why he incessantly rewrote his poetry. "Because I am alive," he responded. His poetry was not of the past, but the present. His poems were not remains of his own history, but creative acts that would continue inflaming his relationship with the world. They were not his legacy but his eyes, lips, veins.

The 1976 publication logically closed a cycle. It included a substantial body of notes accompanying the principal poems. There was a spirit of seeking to come to terms with the past by bringing it into the foreground. In "Pasado en claro," ("A Draft of Shadows") he states, "With words and their shadows I built a moving house of reflections, a walking tower, the construction of windows [...] I am the shadow cast by my words."

3. The Tree and the Forest

After eleven years of not offering any book of poetry to the public (though many essays), in 1987 Octavio Paz published *Árbol adentro* (*A Tree Within*); in this the erotic aspect of his poetry came back in full force, confirming that in reality his whole poetics is a kind of erotism in the sense of a search for the other, of the desired "otherness," and the encounter with it is the tactile surface of the poem. In *Árbol adentro* (*A Tree Within*), melancholy twilights of his earlier poems become new dawns. Friendship, art, memory and the world are all present in this work.

In *Árbol adentro* (*A Tree Within*) everything – such as trees rustling their leaves – becomes a language with which the speaker might communicate with his beloved. Things become signs scattered by the lovers. But alongside the poet's *eros* stands *thanatos*; death accompanies love. The central section of the book is dedicated to life's fleetingness. "Human speech the daughter of death," the poet affirms.

In its first section, *Árbol adentro* (*A Tree Within*) opens with a prologue poem which Paz has entitled Proem and which begins with an affirmation of this duality: "Sometimes poetry is the frenzy of bodies and the frenzy of joy and the frenzy of death..."

The final edition of *Árbol adentro* (*A Tree Within*) in the *Obras completas* (*Complete Works*) opens with a new explanation from the author:

> This book takes the form of a tree with five branches. Its roots are mental; its leaves are syllables. The first branch is oriented toward time and seeks the perfection of the instant. The second speaks with other trees, its distant neighbours. The third contemplates

itself but does not see itself; death is transparent. The fourth is a conversation about painted images, a forest of *living pillars.* The fifth leans over a wellspring and learns words from the beginning.

The concluding section of the book is one of the most beautiful long poems of his work: an "act of faith in love and poetry." The poem's composition takes the form of a cantata with three clearly different sections followed by a coda. The poet's voice opens the canto. In an intermediate time outside of time, in the spirited solitude of the lover, the fleeting materiality of his words appears, and little by little we see the imagined figure of the beloved in the geography of her childhood. The hills of Meknes where Marie José lived as a child. The bird that flies in circles over the houses on the hill and the song of the muezzin, everything dissolved into the siesta of the child who houses the woman of today. In this exceptional time the poet says,

> Neither asleep nor awake:
> You float through a time without hours.
> A breath barely stirs up
> remote countries of mint and wellsprings.
> Let yourself be carried by these words
> back to yourself.

In the second section we move from a single voice to a chorus that, in successive and sometimes opposite ways, defines love. The song becomes a polyphony, and love is a rebellious reality that does not admit restraint. If we see the names in the poem, great thinkers appear. The voices of Plato, Dante, Lope de Vega and many others sing in the font of the visions of love and the ever-mutating couple. In the third part we return to a song in a single voice, that of the poet from the beginning, who now enriches his vision in the agitated flow of the polyphony we have just lived. The poet returns to the themes of the couple and a constantly mutating love. These are joined in the search for that which overtakes us again and again:

> The couple
> is a couple because there is no Eden.
> We are the ones cast out of the Garden,
> condemned to invent it
> and cultivate its delirious flowers,
> living jewels we cut
> to adorn a neck.
> We are condemned
> to leave the Garden:
> before us
> the world awaits.

In the "Coda," the lovers are already moving together through the world, discovering that love entails walking; it entails remaining as still as trees, looking. In this way they complement one another's existence:

> I speak
> because you rustle your leaves.

4. The Incessant Search and Chance

If the variety of languages separates us, secret rivers of words unite poets from all horizons. Passion and curiosity for poetry written in other languages has always led poets to investigate other poetic traditions and find within them astonishing similarities and differences to their own. From those amazements come some notable translations that become the translating poet's own new creations. Already in Paz's first essays on the nature of translation, included in *El signo y el garabato*, Paz explained the ways in which translation and poetic creation are twin processes. He argued that the communicating vessels of both might be full. This politics of translation as a new creation is a good discussion point for those who would see it only as an effort of literal (rather than literary) fidelity. "Translation is not merely transportation, but also transmutation." In this affirmation Paz does not refer to literary works exclusively. "The history of civilization is the history of translations that people have made of the cultures of their ancestors and their neighbours, their enemies and their vassals."

Therefore, in the case of Octavio Paz as translator, each transmutation not only lays the groundwork for a new Spanish poem by Paz that often distances itself significantly from the original in order to become a great poem by Paz, but it also becomes a reflection on the poet and poem being translated, its counterparts in the history of our language or its lack thereof. More than this, at times this reflection becomes a great essay that does not limit itself to the technical problems of translation, but also inserts us into the world of the foreign poet, the poetry of his or her culture and the poetic task in itself. Translation creates the poet. And it makes him or her more lucid, more open and less conformist because it knows that no translation is ever definitive; it can always be improved. Bringing poems to life is a constant challenge.

Paz was a passionate and tireless translator. He also developed some theories about translation, but above all, in Mexico he came to know many poets. One of these was Fernando Pessoa. However he also translated (with help) writers from China and Japan, India and Sweden. In his book *Versiones y diversiones (Versions and Diversions)* (1974) he brought together a good part of his craftsmanship as a translator in about 250 pages including notes. But in his complete works, thirty years later, his *Versiones y diversiones* had multiplied and had come to represent nearly a third of Octavio Paz's poetry. This is why they are included in the *Obra poética* "...beginning with poems in other languages, I sought to create poems in my own."

Here, passion encounters chance. And in none of these books is this more evident than in that of his poetic translations. The translated poems are not the product of some systematic program of diffusion or study, but of invitations, attempts, missions, obsessions. "Passion and chance," says Octavio Paz, "but also, in a word, plumbing work: verbal industry. Poetic translation demands the employment of resources analogous to those of creation, but in a different direction." The creator opens the window to let the bird fly out. The translator opens the window to let the bird come in, change its color, and then leave again to fly through a different window. Thus, translation draws attention to the task of the poet in the otherness of the world; in making it somewhat one's own, the poet makes oneself somewhat other.

In this double transmutation, passion for knowledge is a permanent component of the act of translation. His translation of and essay on John Donne's erotic poem "Elegy: To His Mistress Going to Bed" becomes not only a notable immersion in the sensibility and work of the seventeenth century English poet and his affinities for the Spanish poetry of his time, but also a sensual, brilliant poem that at the end refines four complex lines that the poet included speaking of himself in the third person and concludes with a completely contemporary turn that is Paz's own:

Más allá de la pena y la inocencia
deja caer esa camisa blanca.
Mírame, ven, ¿qué mejor manta
para tu desnudez que yo desnudo?

(cast all, yea, this white linen hence,
There is no penance due to innocence.
To teach thee, I am naked first; why then
What needst thou have more covering than a man?)

(Beyond all shame and innocence
let that white shirt fall down.
Look at me, see, what better covering
for your nakedness than my own?) [1]

His translation of a poem by Apollinaire, "The musician of Saint-Merry," generates an immersion, exploration and explication of the genesis of the poem, its resources of simultaneity, its meanings and mysteries. Something similar happens with many of his translations of other poets. Eikichi Hayashiya, with whom he realizes the translation of *Sendas de Oku* by Matsyo Basho, the understanding that Paz demonstrates and transmits in his essays on *haiku* and Japanese literature is the work of an incessant search over several decades. Ayashiya writes, "On reading it, I felt a great excitement, almost a shiver, when I became aware of the way in which Octavio struggled to translate a Basho poem, meditating on it and searching for adequate words to transmit its true meaning."

Paz was indeed a translator of poetry, but he was always something more. A total translator of a cultural moment and its expressions. One could almost say that in his general work as an essayist, including in his political essays, Octavio Paz acted as one possessed by the same inquisitive, insatiable spirit of the translator that never finishes his or her approach, that is always trying again and again to understand and explore without closing any theme. His work as a literary essayist was also very active in those two decades. He brought together very diverse articles, themes on the margins of reality, in *In/mediaciones* (*In/mediations*) (1979). Essays on art and literature in *Sombras de obras* (*Shadows of works*) (1983) and *Hombres en su siglo* (*Men in their times*) (1984). Enrico Mario Santí rescued his *Primeras letras 1931-1943* (*Early letters 1931-1943*)

---

1 Two English translations are provided here. The first is the original English version of Donne's poem. The second is a translation into English of Paz's translation to reflect the substantial changes made by Paz.

(1988) and Hugo J. Verani found a selection of interviews in *Pasión crítica* (*Critical Passion*) (1983).

In 1974 he had published one of his fundamental books: *Los hijos del limo* (*Children of the Mire*). This was based on the lectures he gave at Harvard in 1972 on literature and the end of the avant gardes, or on

> the double and antagonistic temptation that has alternatively or simultaneously fascinated modern poets: the religious temptation and the political temptation, magic and revolution. Before Christianity modern poetry presents itself as the other religion; before the revolutions of the nineteenth and twentieth centuries, it sets itself as the original revolution. A double heterodoxy, a double tension that is present in the Romantic William Blake, the symbolist Yeats and the avant garde Pound; it is present in Baudelaire as well as Breton, in Pessoa and in Vallejo.

In 1982 he published *Sor Juana Inés de la Cruz o las trampas de la fe* (*Sor Juana Inés de la Cruz or the Traps of Faith*), a biography that is also a study of literary criticism and a book of the history of the vice-royalty of New Spain. A fundamental book of the Mexican literature of today, a study of a living work, a polemical past and vital situations that can clearly be compared with the present. In the first edition Paz explains the need to know Sor Juana's life and world in order to better read her work in the present. He calls his essay "an attempt at restitution." Once again in the work of Octavio Paz, we hear of a reflection on the complex and contradictory, passionate and multiform place of poetry in history and the history of literary work.

In 1987 there appeared in three thick volumes a selection of the work of Octavio Paz on Mexico. The first of these, *El peregrino en su patria* (*The Pilgrim in His Homeland*), compiles a full selection of his articles on the history and politics of Mexico. The second, *Generaciones y semblanzas* (*Genealogies and Biographies*), brings together essays on literature and Mexican writers. Both were edited by Luis Mario Schneider and the author, taking the 1979 edition that included both of them as their base. The third, completely selected by Octavio Paz, is called *Los privilegios de la vista* (*The Privileges of Sight*) and is the most unusual: it presents a rich collection of essays on Mexican art that had never before appeared together; topics include pre-Hispanic art, nineteenth century art, criticism and a re-evaluation of some aspects of the muralist movement, and contemporary artists. In these three books, as is his custom, Paz rewrites, re-edits, adds new texts, reflects on the meanings of what he has done and what he still needs to do. The three volumes went up for sale under the title *Mexico in the work of Octavio Paz,* and this later formed the basis for a series of twelve television programs.

Octavio Paz worked with a certain frequency making cultural programs for Mexican television. Among these are *Conversaciones con Octavio Paz* (*Conversations with Octavio Paz*) (1984), a series on Ezra Pound in 1986, the series *México en la obra de Octavio Paz* (*Mexico in the Work of Octavio Paz*) (1989) and the political series *El siglo XX: la experiencia de la libertad* (*The Twentieth Century: The Experience of Freedom*) (1990). Again taking up the title *Los privilegios de la vista* (*The Privileges of Sight*), he organized in 1990, in the Mexico City museum, el Centro Cultural/Arte Contemporáneo, a great exposition bringing together different works of art that, like stars guiding one's vision, have influenced the poet throughout his life. After nearly fifty years after writing about art these become evidence in a full, varied explanation. A voluminous catalogue entitled *Octavio Paz: los privilegios de la vista* (*Octavio Paz: the Privileges of sight*), reproduced part of the work and presented essays by Paz on art as well as various essays about Paz and the visual arts. In this exposition the collages of Marie

José Paz were shown for the first time. A new essay on the arts of Mexico, "Voluntad de forma" ("The Will of Form") opens the catalogue of the monumental exposition *México: esplendores de treinta sigos* (*Mexico: The Splendours of Thirty Centuries*), presented in the Metropolitan Museum of Art in New York in 1990. Paz gave various lectures and poetry readings in New York in conjunction with this event.

The theme of the place of poetry in society and history would reappear in his work *La otra voz. Poesía y fin de siglo* (*The Other Voice: Poetry and the End of the Century*) (1990). This includes essays on the nature and history of the long poem as a manifestation of the contemporary world, as well as a study of modernity, myth and the revolution in his relationship with the work of poetry. It also signals his desire to experiment, more in the background than that archived in *Blanco* (*White*), with audiovisual methods of creating poems. It is significant that in his prologue Paz situates this essay as a culmination of a reflexive essay on poetry that began nearly fifty years earlier in his first essay on poetic experience, that continued in *El arco y la lira* (*The Bow and the Lyre*) in the 1950's, in many essays isolated and in *Los hijos del limo* (*Children of the Mire*) during the 1970's. In 1990 he would again ask himself in many ways about the future of poetry. "More than a description and less than a prophecy, my response is a profession of faith. These pages," the poet says, "are nothing but one more variation on that 'Defence of Poetry' that for more than two centuries the modern poets have been writing tirelessly. Now threatened by the blind logic of the market (which now occupies the role previously held by religions and political ideologies) poetry is the most radical "other voice" that allows us to reconcile ourselves with our human condition."

Its voice is "other" because it is the voice of passion and vision; it is from another world and this world; it is ancient but from this time, antiquity without dates.

A poetry that is heretical and schismatic, innocent and perverse, clear and muddy, aerial and underground, poetry of the hermitage and the corner bar, poetry at arm's reach and of a world beyond that is always here already.

Paz also expresses concern for the possible function of poetry:

One can say without exaggeration that the theme of the end of this century is not that of political organization of our societies nor their historical orientation. Today, the urgency lies in knowing how we are going to ensure the survival of the human species. Facing this reality, what might be the function of poetry? What can the other voice say? I have already indicated that if a new form of political thought arises, its influence will be indirect: to remember certain realities that have been buried, to bring them to life and reveal them. Before the question of the survival of humanity in a poisoned, destroyed land, the response cannot be any different. Its influence will be indirect: to suggest, inspire, and insinuate. Not to prove, but to reveal.

The appearance of this "Defence of Poetry" in Mexican bookstores coincided with Paz's receipt of the Nobel Prize for Literature. The news reached him during his stay in New York, and he received the prize two months later in Sweden, in December of 1990.

VI
In the Spiral
The Search for the Present
1990-1998

1. The Fellowship of the Present

The Swedish Academy declared that it was awarding the 1990 Nobel Prize for Literature to Octavio Paz "for his passionate writing of many horizons, characterized by his sensual intelligence and humanistic integrity."

A few weeks later, on December 10, Kjell Espmark, the person tasked with introducing Paz during the awarding of the prize, tried to define him in two words: passion and integrity. "Both of these are united in the energetic *non serviam*, the firm refusal to serve that this poet directed toward various factions." He mentions Paz's opposition to the totalitarian powers of Stalinism, the unethical, anti-cultural powers of capitalism, and also his resignation from diplomatic service in 1968 following the massacre of Tlatelolco. Espmark also praised the visible passion in a rare synthesis of "thought and sensuality" that he found in Paz's poetry and reflections on poetry.

During the banquet that followed the Nobel award ceremony, before a thousand guests, each prizewinner was expected to raise a three-minute toast offering a glimpse of the meaning of his or her work. In his "Nobel toast," Paz briefly returned to some of the questions and topics developed in *La otra voz* (*The Other Voice*) and turned them into a manifesto for fellowship and the powers of poetry.

> We are living not only at the end of a century but of
> a historical period. What will come from the collapse

of ideologies? Is this the dawning of a new age of universal harmony and freedom for all, or will we see the
return of tribal ideologies and religious fanaticism
with its trail of all kinds of discord and tyranny? Will
the powerful democracies that have amassed an abun-
dance of wealth in a state of freedom become less ego-
tistical and more understanding of the dispossessed
nations? Will these impoverished nations learn to
mistrust the violent, dogmatic ones who have brought
catastrophe to them? In my part of the world, Latin
America, and especially in Mexico, my country, will
we reach the goal of true modernity, which is not only
political democracy, economic prosperity and social
justice but a reconciliation with our tradition and with
our very selves?

According to Paz, among all the questions for which we still
don't have answers, a sole certainty imposes itself upon us:
the threat to the life of our planet. "The defence of nature is
the defence of humanity." He also returns to the theme of the
poet's vocation at the end of the century, but instead of revealing and developing the idea, as he did in *La otra voz* (*The Other
Voice*), he tried to go a little beyond that, presenting and reading a short poem from *Árbol adentro* (*A Tree Within*), "Stars
and crickets," where the macrocosm and microcosm correspond to one another.

Upon finishing this century, we have discovered that
we are part of an immense system, or a set of systems,
that extends from animals and plants to cells, mole-
cules, atoms and stars. We are one link in the "Great
Chain of Being," as ancient philosophers referred to the
universe. One of the oldest gestures of human beings,
repeated daily from the beginning of time, is to raise
one's head and contemplate the starry sky in a state of

wonder. This contemplation almost always ends with a feeling of communion with the universe. Many years ago, one night in the country, as I was contemplating a sky that was pure and filled with stars, I heard among the dark grasses the metallic song of a cricket's wings. There was a strange correspondence between the nocturnal palpitations of the firmament and the tiny music of the insect. I wrote the following lines:

The heavens are vast
and worlds are being planted above.
Impassive
the carpenter cricket
proceeds through that night.

Stars, hills, clouds, trees, birds, crickets, human beings: each one alone in its world, each one a world; nevertheless, all these different worlds correspond to one another. Only if we renew among ourselves the feeling of belonging to nature will we be able to defend life. It is not impossible: fraternity is a word that belongs to the liberal tradition as well as the socialist one, the scientific tradition and the religious one.

It is the custom of the Nobel Lecture, obviously longer than the speech given on the day of the awards ceremony, to be given another day before a smaller audience. Thus, two days before the large ceremony, on December 8, Octavio Paz read his at the Swedish Academy of Literature. "La búsqueda del presente" ("The Search for the Present") this a very important essay because Paz tries to put the key moments of his vocation into perspective and to continue unraveling the meaning of his life as a writer and indeed the very meaning of writing at the end of the century. He begins by signaling the situation of Hispanic American literature's oddness compared to the Spanish literary tradition. And upon this he constructs a personal testimony of the "feeling of separation" from reality and the exclusion from the present state of the world that he experiences again and again. "Up to now I have hardly understood that among what I call my expulsion from the present and my writing of poetry there was a secret relationship."

Therefore, writing is part of Paz's search for the present. A search that Paz later explains is a search for modernity. And he examines the collapse of those ideas of modernity that believed in a future whose development could be known in advance. Thus, he criticizes the capitalist idea of progress as well as the utopian socialist idea of an ideal society. History has sent both of those tumbling down, and the future is even more difficult to foresee.

"For a very long time I have firmly believed that the decline of the future is announced in the coming of today." And, in response to the decline of the philosophies of the future, Paz proposes and announces the possibility of developing a philosophy of the present. "To think of today means, above all else, to recharge the critical gaze." The currently triumphant market economy needs to be criticized and weighed with fresh eyes. And the necessary critique of the triumphant market economy should signal that market's responsibility for the world's ecological problems. The very survival of the planet is at stake. According to Paz, it would be good if poetic experience, poetic philosophy could be considered one of the bases of that search, that new philosophy of today.

With this idea there arises a revelation of the instant but also an awareness of transience:

> In my pilgrimage in search of modernity I lost and found myself many times. I returned to my roots and discovered that modernity is not outside ourselves but inside. It is today and it is the most ancient antiquity. It is tomorrow and the beginning of the world; it is a

thousand years old and has just been born [...] It is the instant, that bird that is everywhere and nowhere. We want to grasp it alive but it opens its wings and unfolds, transformed into a fistful of syllables. We remain with our hands empty. Then the doors of perception open part way and another kind of time appears, the true kind that we seek without realizing it: the present, presence.

It's significant that in his Nobel Lecture, which is simultaneously a manifesto for the present moment, Paz finishes by speaking of the fleetingness of the instant and the fleetingness of all certainties. That feeling of transience also extends to a way of facing death squarely and also facing the fragility of our sense of life. This double sensation, it seems to me, is at the origin of the enormous writing and publishing efforts that would occupy Paz in the following years.

Starting at the end of the 1980's Paz concentrated on editing his complete works, revising everything, rewriting it with the intention of improving upon it, creating a retrospective composition but at the same time updating what he had written throughout his life. The project had its origin in the Círculo de Lectores (Circle of Readers) publishing house in Barcelona, which at the time was directed by Heinz Meinke. A first edition was just for the members of the club, purchased though a prior subscription; another almost simultaneous edition was sold to the general public under the "Galaxia Gutenberg" (Gutenberg Galaxy) imprint. The Colombian poet Nicanor Vélez, from Barcelona, worked with Paz daily on the project. And in Mexico it was published in full by the Fondo de Cultura Económica. The first edition was made in fifteen volumes, 8,338 pages in a large format. The definitive edition integrated his final writings in their thematic order; this one had eight volumes with 10,213 pages in total.

In 1988 Meinke informed me of his desire to take advantage of Octavio Paz's editorial experience to give order to this enormous, multiform, ever-changing work. He told me of the author's hesitation to embark on this kind of project, and also his final commitment. This would be a nearly total immersion during little less than a decade. The diversity and quantity of the work was already intimidating. But the very challenge of giving shape to diversity was an interesting goal for the author. Many years earlier he had written an observation about Alfonso Reyes that could now be applied to himself:

> The work of Reyes is disconcerting not only due to its length but also due to the variety of issues it deals with; however, it is far from being scattered. Everything tends toward synthesis, including that part of his production constituted by notes, commentaries on and summaries of distant books. In a period of discord and uniformity, two sides of the same coin, Reyes puts forth a will toward coherence, the search for an order that does not exclude the singularity of its parts.

This "will toward coherence" would mark the poet's final years.

2. Retrospective Glance

As this search for the meaning of life and of his work would imply writing prologues for each one of the numerous volumes that he was forming, the texts that signal, warn, offer clues, lament that which has not been done and bring the dispersed things together constitute a declaration of principles about the entire body of work. A retrospective composition that would be collected in 2002 into a posthumous volume aptly named *Por las sendas de la memoria* (*On the Paths of Memory*). The first of his prologues is from April 1990, and it signals the character of his now explicit search for coherence. This is not separate from the very character of his writing:

> I have written and I continue to write moved by con-
> trary impulses: from a desire to penetrate myself and
> flee from myself, from love of life and the desire to
> seek revenge against it, from a yearning for commu-
> nion and the desire to earn a few cents, from a longing
> to preserve the gesture of a loved one and to converse
> with a stranger, from the desire for perfection and the
> need to get things off my chest, to stop the instant and
> send it flying again. In sum, to live and survive. There-
> fore, because I am still alive now, I am writing these
> lines. Will I survive? I don't know, nor does it matter
> to me. The yearning for survival is perhaps a madness,
> but it is an innate, common, inextinguishable madness.
> Beyond my salvation or my loss in another world, I will
> say that in writing I placed my bets on the most fragile,
> precious human faculty: memory.

The door to Paz's poetry would be his reflection on that poetry and on poetry's place in the world. Thus, the first volume was entitled *La casa de la presencia: poesía e historia* (*The House of Presence: Poetry and History*).

> Poetry exorcises the past: in this way, the present be-
> comes habitable. All times, from the mythic time as
> long as a millennium to the lightning flash of an instant,
> becomes the present when touched by poetry. What
> happens in a poem is the fall of Troy or the precarious
> embrace of lovers; both are always taking place. The
> present of poetry is a transfiguration: time is incarnat-
> ed in a presence. The poem is the home of presence.
> Words made from air are woven together; the poem is
> infinitely fragile and nevertheless infinitely resistant. It
> is a perpetual challenge to the weight of history.

The following volumes were then dedicated to his abundant writings on global, Hispanic and Mexican literature. Then came the writings on universal and Mexican art. The eighth volume was devoted to the history and politics of Mexico. The prologue, dated December 1992, "Entrada retrospectiva" ("Retrospective Entrance") is already an explicit memoir of his passion for Mexico. It evokes his childhood and youth, his feelings of exclusion, the challenges that history kept presenting and, always, the new challenges.

But it is evident that Paz was not satisfied with this memoir because, when he presented his essays on world history and politics the following year, he included a kind of continuation of the memoir that would keep on growing until it became a kind of political autobiography: *Itinerario* (*Itinerary*), a new book within the book. In this Paz reviewed his life, the key historic moments and his position with respect to them. A personal history of his ideas, his political and social opinions. It ends with a reflection on the present and his desire for a new political philosophy that would form a bridge between philosophical reflection and scientific knowledge, particularly physics. A reflection that also would consider and include poetry and literature in its reflections. "No one should dare to write on themes of philosophy or political theory without having read and meditated upon the Greek tragedians and Shakespeare, Dante and Cervantes, Balzac and Dostoevsky." At the end of his *Itinerario* (*Itinerary*), speaking in terms very similar to those of his Nobel toast, he returned to the theme of a necessary critique of the market and the need to construct a true fellowship. He concluded that in the moment of writing that memoir he was invaded by the same feeling he had in 1929, that of dissatisfaction with the modern world and a sense of the need to change it.

3. Return to India with Parvati

The edition of Paz's complete works again and again provoked in Paz the uncomfortable sense that he still had a lot to write. He was living in the twilight of the possible. The urgent need to respond to promises he had made over many years. And while he brought together his essays on history and international politics and cultures and otherness in *Ideas y costumbres* (*Ideas and Customs*), he felt that he had not finished his reflection on the experience of love. Thus, in the heart of his complete works, he felt the need for a new book that was burning in his throat: *La llama doble, amor y erotismo* (*The Double Flame, Love and Erotism*).

For many years Paz spoke of his desire to write a long essay on the experience of love, which had partially advanced and that in his original plan had five volumes. These were ultimately condensed into one. He says that he had started wanting to write this essay when he fell in love in India in the 1960's. And from that point forward he took notes and developed ideas, slowly building the work without diving completely into editing it. His recent long poem on love, *Carta de creencia* (*Act of Faith*), would be the antecedent and poetic counterpart of this new book. But so would many of his love poems written since the 60's, where his reflections appear and reappear, transformed into images "like recurrent musical phrases."

Written compulsively in a few months, *La llama doble* (*The Double Flame*) is simultaneously a natural history of the idea of love in various civilizations, a painstaking examination into the meaning of love, and an intense reading of love poetry from many different times. It is also a vital synthesis that makes us experience the author's liveliness as we accompany him in his readings (or while he accompanies us in the readings that he invites us to). His presence, particularly in this essay, is of an intensity similar to that which we feel in his poems and his reflections on those poems. His investigation of the idea and sentiment of love in various cultures is immense, but it was made over an entire lifetime. It was radically lived. Perhaps for this reason *La llama doble* (*The Double Flame*) is one of the magnetic centres of Octavio Paz's work as an essayist.

Paz invites us not to confuse sexuality with eroticism and love. Sex is fuller and less complex. It is a manifestation of life in its many forms.

> Eroticism is exclusively human; it is sexuality that has been socialized and transfigured by the imagination and will of human beings. Love is attraction toward one person, a body and a soul. Love is an act of choosing; eroticism is accepting. Without eroticism, without a visible form by which it enters the senses, there is no love, but love goes beyond the desired body and seeks the soul inside that body, and the body inside the soul. It seeks the entire person.

If fire is sex, from it grows a double flame made by love and eroticism.

The book on love, which is also a bird's eye view of the best of many civilizations, leads to a reflection on the contemporary world, the meaning of history, new scientific viewpoints on life, and the necessary reconstruction of the idea of the "human person." A fight against the economic and political wrongs of society, but also against the moral and spiritual wrongs, which are no less urgent.

While preparing this same volume of *Obras completas* (*Complete Works*) that provoked the writing of *La llama doble* (*The Double Flame*), Octavio Paz let himself be invaded by another urgency, the necessity of paying another of his debts. He decided to write his ideas and memories from the country where he had lived for six years, the place where he had fallen in love and then resigned from his job as a diplomat in rebellion against his government. The country where his life and work took an unusual turn. He called it *Vislumbres de la India* (*Glimpses of India*).

If *La llama doble* (*The Double Flame*) had its origin in his love for Marie José Paz, which began in India, this book on India contains an important section on love. The books are closely related in their secret passage toward passion.

"The fact of being Mexican," says Paz, "helped me to see India's differences from the perspective of my own differences as a Mexican. They are not the same, of course, but they offer a point of view." Paz invites us to take part in his already long, intense, loving dialogue with India. This country transformed him, and everything he wrote afterwards bears its mark in one way or another.

Thus, erotism is not only an important theme. Due to his experience with India, Paz's poetics became an erotic discourse.

"In India," says Paz, "I encounter a fabric of sensations, ideas, and experiences. Erotism, for example, neither draws me closer nor distances me from the sacred. An experience that for a Westerner is very difficult. Erotism is sexuality transformed by imagination. Love in this erotic imagination is transformed into the selection of one person. And that is what I discovered in India, a discovery that probably changed my poetry. On the one hand it gave more reality, more density to my words; they became fuller, more pregnant with meaning. On the other hand, they became more lucid. This was, in a certain sense, a recovery of the reality of his world through the beloved person."

The scene in which Paz relates his discovery of India like a sensory initiation is very significant and revealing. This was the visit to the caves on Elephanta Island.

We walked along a grey and red path that led us to the mouth of an immense cave. I entered a world made of shadows interrupted by sudden clarities. The patterns of light, the fullness of the spaces and their irregular forms, the figures carved into the walls gave the place a sacred character, in the deepest sense of the word. Among the shadows I saw reliefs and powerful statues, many of them mutilated by the fanatic jealousy of Portuguese colonizers and Muslims, but all of then majestic, solid, made of a solar material. Physical beauty transformed into living stone. Divinities of the earth, sexual embodiments of the most abstract thought, gods simultaneously intellectual and bodily, terrible and peaceful. Shiva smiles from a beyond in which time is a drifting little cloud, and suddenly, that cloud becomes dripping water, and then that water becomes the thin young girl who is spring itself: the goddess Parvati. The divine couple is the image of happiness that our mortal condition offers us, only to take it away an instant later. That palpable, tangible, eternal world is not for us. There is a vision of happiness simultaneously terrestrial and unreachable. Thus began my initiation into the art of India.

In *Vislumbres de la India* I see the realization of a concept that I have always noticed when reading Indian art historians (like Coomaraswamy): they state frequently state that a given work has (or does not have) "Rasha." My understanding is that Rasha is the grace of a work, but also its essence, understood not only as content but as flavour, taste, and a certain depth. Rasha is analyzed in the theories of theatre as an expressive force that a work has to produce different states or feelings in its spectators. Those sentiments are normally classified in nine categories. (There is a reason why Paz believes that Indians

have a passion for infinite classifications, for subtle differences, as exemplified in the Kama Sutra. The central Rasha,
Rasharajá, or the king of aesthetic sensibilities, is the erotic
sense (Shringara). All the other aesthetic senses are connect-
ed in one way or another with this one.

The erotic sense, seen in this way, as a sensitive thought,
is a key to obtaining the delights of reason. In other words,
it is an exercise filled with reason, never separated from the
senses. And, it seems to me, it is one more key toward an understanding of the work of Octavio Paz in all its dimensions
and themes. It's the backbone of his concert.

4. The fragility of life

When Paz's *Ideas y costumbres II* (*Ideas and Customs II*) was
finally published in 1996, with a relative delay in comparison
to the rhythm with which his previous volumes had appeared,
it offered a presentation of Paz's work that made a deep impression on his readers. He said the reasons for the delay were
"accidental but nevertheless inevitable." The harshest, most
terrible of these was the following:

> and when I set out to complete my tasks, in particularly
> the prologue to this book, an uninvited guest knocked
> on my door: illness. I opened it, and without a word,
> illness gave me a look that ran over me, but which I
> cannot define: it was neither anger nor pity nor even
> indifference. It was what we call, in our lack of ability
> to say what we truly feel, suffering. After a few days
> the doctors decoded the meaning of that gaze for me:
> I had a mortal wound, and if I wanted to escape from
> it, I would need a severe operation. After a few days of
> doubt, I discussed it with my wife and decided to try it.

At the age of eighty, at a very high risk, Paz decided to subject himself to an open heart surgery.

The operation was successful. And that same year the volume appeared with his prologue, *Nosotros los otros* (*We the Others*). He also published the first volume of his *Obra poética* (*Poetic Works*). Alas, this was to be the definitive version of his poetry. Until that point, eleven volumes of fifteen had been edited. There was still a lot to add. After preparing the second volume of his poetic work it would be necessary to compile his earlier works, the various works of his later years, and a selection of interviews. But at the end of 1996, while he was convalescent, a fire destroyed the main hall of Octavio and Marie José Paz's home. In that space they kept their most costly items, particularly objects from India, Pakistan and Afghanistan. These were the most meaningful artifacts from the beginning of their common adventure in life. There were also various paintings given to them by friends, including Roberto Matta and Juan Soriano. The books that they had kept from the library of Paz's grandfather and a collection of first editions. Meanwhile, around this time Paz was diagnosed with a very aggressive form of cancer. With the same vitality with which a few years earlier he had faced a serious heart operation, he now faced this cancer.

Soon afterwards, in full awareness of the seriousness of his illness, symbolically closing another circle in his life, in one of the final versions of his *Obras completas* he presented these first words:

> I am writing this at the end of my days. This volume contains all the efforts of a novice writer [...] the discoveries, affinities, negations and, at the end, all the loves and hates of a young Mexican writer fed and formed by the avant garde but who, at the middle of the century, sought to explore other avenues [...] The impulse that led me to correct some of my poems has been a dissatisfaction before my works and their de-

fects. I corrected and eliminated certain parts not for sordid ideological reasons, but rather from my thirst for perfection. I have not been the only one to do this: an infinity of writers have felt the same way and done similarly to me.

This sunset text deals with the dawning of the poet. "The calling and the learning" are the two wings of the bird of a literary vocation. He tells of how he experienced the mystery of the call to become a writer, how he obeyed that call, and what accidental course gave him training in the vocation.

A little before that, still in 1996, he wrote a short text, "Preliminar II" ("Preliminary II") as a prologue to the second volume of his poetic works, which in principle would include everything written from 1969 to 1996, with all his translations and collaborative poems. Here there is a clear warning: "The true biography of a poet does not lie in life events, but in poems. The events are the *materia prima*, the raw material; what we read is a poem, a re-creation (at times a negation) of this or that experience [...] The poems are not confessions but revelations." Thus, in his poem "Respuesta y reconciliación" ("Response and Reconciliation") he concludes,

And while I saw what I say,
time and space are falling,
dizzily, restlessly. They fall into themselves.
The human person and the galaxy return to silence.
Does it matter? Yes – but it doesn't matter:
we already know that silence is music
and we are one chord of the concert.

Octavio Paz died in Mexico City on April 19, 1998, almost two weeks after his eighty-fourth birthday. In one of his poems he had written the following:

Burial is still baroque
in Mexico
    To die is still to die
at some time in some place

To close one's eyes on a white day
a day never seen any day
now your eyes will see and mine will not.

The poetry, essays, political analysis, polemic, editing, translation, and active cultural promotion that Paz realized over a
period of more than sixty-five years of writing is one of the
most profound, varied and lucid footprints to mark the face
of twentieth century culture, in Mexico and across the world.
His lucidity remains fertile; he revealed a tenacious way of en-
acting criticism within creation and creation within criticism.

He also showed the way, in which, starting with poetry, the
disciplines of historical reflection, politics, and anthropolo-
gy might be deepened, given more dimensions, and a greater
space for rebellion.

He also gave us, in his poems, many entrances into the
depths of ourselves and others. He gave us the password to
what he called "our small ration of eternity." The greatest
antidote and challenge of human beings to the density and
opaqueness of society, politics and history.

VII. Coda
The Noonday Tree

Revelation of the Instant

In a long interview with Octavio Paz about his life and work we discussed his poem "Pasado en claro," ("A Draft of Shadows") which he described as an "attempt to see my childhood and early adolescence [...] Because I believe that the child is the seed of the creation of the human being. Everything we make is already present in the child, and what matters in each human life is to be worthy of the child that we were, to realize that human prophecy that each child is.".

Later, commenting on the nocturnal character of his poem, Octavio Paz expressed what for him is one of the senses of poetry. And without meaning to, he spoke to us of the luminous but fleeting sense of a life dedicated to poetry. But also, the meaning that our life acquires upon reading that poetry, if we are lucky enough to live it as a revelation.

> "Pasado en claro" ("A Draft of Shadows") is a nocturne, that is certain. I had not thought of it in that way. But I would like to add something. That poem ends with an evocation and convocation of noon. A noon that is more mental than actually lived, for the poem comes face to face with the idea of death: we are mortal, we are made of time and history. Are there any ways out of history other than death? I ask myself this in a given moment, and then I remember what we might call noon: that unique moment when time dissolves, a way

out of history and death. Time, though it continues
to pass, seems to stand still. It is the window toward
eternity that each human has. An experience that the
mystics expressed very well. But it is not necessary to
be a saint or a mystic to have that experience. I believe
that all humans, all children, sometimes people in love,
all of us who stand looking at the twilight, or looking at
a painting, or looking at a tree, or looking at nothing,
just looking at a wall, we experience those moments in
which time disappears, dissolves: those great human
moments that are a human being's way out. This is
what I call our small ration of eternity.

I don't know what else we have, but there is something we
do have, something that poetry claims. If people were to read
more poetry in this century, maybe it would be easier to reach
these instants. Not because poetry creates them, but because
it reveals them. "Pasado en claro"("A Draft of Shadows") is a
nocturne, it is true, but from its core the midday tree suddenly
springs forth.

BIBLIOGRAPHY

The most complete bibliography of books by and about Octavio Paz is: Hugo J. Verani, *Bibliografía crítica (1931-2013)* (*Critical Bibliography, 1931-2013*), 3rd edition, Mexico, El Colegio Nacional, 2014, two volumes.

Poetry

Luna silvestre (*Wild Moon*), Fábula, Mexico, 1933.

¡No pasarán! (*They Shall Not Pass!*), Simbad, Mexico, 1936.

Raiz del hombre (*Root of Man*), Simbad, Mexico, 1937.

Bajo tu clara sombra y otros poemas sobre España (*Under Your Clear Shadow and Other Poems on Spain*), Ediciones Españolas, Valencia, 1937.

Entre la piedra y la flor (*Between the Stone and the Flower*), Nueva Voz, Mexico, 1941.

A la orilla del mundo y Primer dia, Bajo tu clara sombra, Raiz del hombre, Noche de resurrecciones, (*At the Shore of the World and First day, Under Your Clear Shadow, Root of Man, Night of Resurrections*) ARS, Mexico,1942.

Libertad bajo palabra*, Tezontle, Mexico, 1949.

Semillas para un himno (*Seeds for a Hymn*), Tezontle, Mexico, 1954.

Piedra de Sol (*Sunstone*), Tezontle, Mexico, 1957.

La estación violenta (*The Violent Season*), Fonda de Cultura Económica, Mexico, 1958.

Libertad bajo palabra: obra poética (*1935-1957*) (*Libertad bajo palabra: Poetic Works*), Fondo de Cultura Economica, México, 1960.*

Salamandra (*Salamander*) (*1958-1961*), Joaquín Mortiz, Mexico, 1962.

Viento entero (*Wind from all Compass Points*)*,* The Caxton Press, Delhi, 1965.

Blanco (*White*), Joaquín Mortiz, Mexico, 1967. Discos visuales, Era, Mexico, 1968.

Discos visuales (*Visual Discs*), Era, Mexico, 1968.

Ladera este (*East Slope*) (*1962-1968*), Joaquín Mortiz, Mexico, 1969.

Topoemas (*Topoems*), Era, Mexico, 1971.

Vuelta (*Return*), El Mendrugo, Mexico, 1971.

Renga (*Renga*), Joaquín Mortiz, Mexico, 1972. A collaborative poem in four languages by Jacques Roubaud, Edoardo Sanguineti, Charles Tomlinson and Octavio Paz.

Versiones y diversiones (*Versions and Diversions*), Joaquín Mortiz, Mexico, 1974.

Pasado en claro (*A Draft of Shadows*), Fondo de Cultura Económica, Mexico, 1975.

Vuelta (*Returns*), Seix Barral, Barcelona, 1976.

Air Born/Hijos del aire, with Charles Tomlinson. Martín Pescador Workshop, Mexico, 1979.

Poemas 1935-1975 (*Poems 1935-1975*), Seix Barral, Barcelona, 1979

Carta de creencia (*Act of Faith*), Papeles Privados, Mexico, 1987.

Árbol adentro (*A Tree Within*), Seix Barral, Barcelona, 1987.
Obra poética 1935-1988 (*Poetic Works 1935-1988*), Seix Barral, Barcelona, 1990.

Figuras y figuraciones (*Figures and Figurations*), with Marie José Paz, Galaxia Gutenberg, Barcelona, 1990.

Reflejos, replicas: diálogos con Francisco de Quevedo (*Reflections, replicas: dialogues with Francisco de Quevedo*), Vuelta / El Colegio Nacional, Mexico, 1996.

* See Translator's Note for a discussion of this title.

Poetry in Prose

¿Águila o sol? (*Eagle or Sun?*), Tezontle, Mexico, 1951.

El mono gramático (*The Grammarian Monkey*), Seix Barral, Barcelona, 1974.

Essays

El laberinto de la soledad (*The Labyrinth of Solitude*), Cuadernos Americanos, Mexico, 1950; Fondo de Cultura Económica, Mexico, 1959.

El arco y la lira (*The Bow and the Lyre*), Fondo de Cultura Económica, Mexico, 1956.

Las peras del alma (*The Pears of the Elm Tree*), Universidad Nacional Autónoma de Mexico, Mexico, 1957.

Cuadrivio (*Quadrivium*), Joaquín Mortiz, Mexico, 1965.

Los signos en rotación (*Signs in Rotation*), Sur, Buenos Aires, 1965.

Puertas al campo (*Doors to the Country*), Universidad Nacional Autónoma de Mexico, Mexico, 1966.

Claude Levi-Strauss o el nuevo festín de Esopo (*Claude Levi-Strauss or the New Feast of Aesop*), Joaquín Mortiz, Mexico,

1967.

Corriente alterna (*Alternating Current*), Siglo XXI Editores, Mexico, 1967.

Marcel Duchamp o el castillo de la pureza (*Marcel Duchamp, or the Castle of Purity*), Era, Mexico, 1968.

Conjunciones y disyunciones (*Conjunctions and Disjunctions*), Joaquín Mortiz, Mexico, 1969.

México: la última década (*Mexico: the Last Decade*), University Press, Austin, 1969.

Posdata (*Postscript*), Siglo XXI Editores, Mexico, 1970.

Las cosas en su sitio: sabre la literatura española (*Things in Their Place: on Spanish Literature*) in collaboration with Juan Marichal. Finisterre, Mexico, 1971.

Traduccion: literatura y literalidad (*Translation: Literature and Literality*). Tusquets, Barcelona, 1971.

Apariencia desnuda: la obra de Marcel Duchamp (*Marcel Duchamp: Appearance Stripped Bare*). Era, Mexico. 1973.

Los hijos del limo: del romanticismo a la vanguardia (*Children of the Mire: Modern Poetry from Romanticism to the Avant-garde*). Seix Barral, Barcelona, 1974.

Xavier Villaurrutia en persona y en obra (*Xavier Villaurrutia: the Man and his Works*), Fondo de Cultura Económica, Mexico, 1978.

El ogro filantropico: historia y politica, 1971-1978 (*The Philanthropic Ogre: History and Politics, 1971-1978*), Joaquín Mortiz, Mexico, 1979.

In/Mediaciones (*In/Mediations*), Seix Barral, Barcelona, 1979.

El laberinto de la soledad, Posdata, Vuelta a El laberinto de la soledad (*The Labyrinth of Solitude, Postscript, Return to the Labyrinth of Solitude*), Fondo de Cultura Económica, Mexico, 1981.

Sor Juana Inés de la Cruz, o las trampas de la fe (*Sor Juana Inés de la Cruz, or the Traps of Faith*), Seix Barral, Barcelona, 1982.

Tiempo nublado (*Cloudy Weather*), Seix Barral, Barcelona, 1983.

Sombras de obras: arte y literatura (*Shadows of Works: Art and Literature*), Seix Barral, Barcelona, 1983.

Hombres en su siglo y otros ensayos (*Men in their Times and Other Essays*), Seix Barral, Barcelona, 1984.

Primeras letras (1931-1943) (*Early Letters, 1931-1943*), Enrico Mario Santí, editor, Vuelta, Mexico, 1988.

Poesía, mito, revolución (*Poetry, Myth, Revolution*), Vuelta, Mexico, 1989.

Pequeña crónica de grandes días (*A Small Chronicle of Grand Days*), Fondo de Cultura Económica, México, 1990.

La otra voz: poesia y fin de siglo (*The Other Voice: Poetry and the End of the Century*), Seix Barral, Barcelona. 1990.

Convergencias (*Convergences*), Seix Barral, Barcelona, 1991.

La búsqueda del presente: fraternidad con la naturaleza (*The Search for the Present: Fraternity with Nature*), Círculo de Lectores, Barcelona, 1991 (Nobel Lecture).

Elogio de la negación (*In Praise of Negation*), Círculo de Lectores, Barcelona, 1992. (Lecture, Frankfurt Book Fair).

Al paso (*On the Way*), Seix Barral, Barcelona, 1992.

Itinerario (*Itinerary*), Fondo de Cultura Economica, Mexico, 1993.

La llama doble: amor y erotismo (*The Double Flame: Love and Erotism*), Seix Barral, Barcelona, 1993.

Un más allá erótico: Sade (*An Erotic Beyond: Sade*), Vuelta/Heliópolis, Mexico, 1994.

Vislumbres de la India (*Glimpses of India*), Seix Barral, Barcelona, 1995.

Estrella de tres puntas: Andre Breton y el surrealismo (*Three-Pointed Star: Andre Breton and Surrealism*), Vuelta, Mexico, 1996.

Pasión crítica (Critical Passion), Hugo J. Verani, Ed., Seix Barral, Barcelona, 1985.

Crónica trunca de días excepcionales (*Short Chronicle of Exceptional days*), Universidad Nacional Autónoma de México, Mexico, 2007.

Por las sendas de la memoria: prologos a una obra (*Though the Paths of Memory: Prologues to a Work*), Galaxia Gutenberg/ Círculo de Lectores, Barcelona, 2002.

Theatre

"La hija de Rappaccini" ("Rappaccini's Daughter"), Revista Mexicana de Literatura, vol. 2, no. 7, September-October 1956; Era, Mexico, 1990.

Complete Works

There are two versions of the complete works. The first is in fifteen volumes and the second, considered the definitive one, in eight. The last miscellaneous writings from the final volume of the first edition have been reclassified within a special dossier in the second.

Obras completas de Octavio Paz (Complete Works of Octavio Paz), author's edition, Círculo de Lectores, Barcelona, and Fondo de Cultura Económica, Mexico, 1991-2004. The first year of each volume corresponds to its publication in Spain; the second, to its publication in Mexico.

I. *La casa de la presencia: poesía e historia* (*The House of Presence: Poetry and History*), *1991 and 1994.*

II. *Excursiones/incursiones: dominio extranjero* (*Excursions/Incursions: Foreign Domain*), 1991 and 1994.

III. *Fundación y disidencia: dominio hispánico* (*Foundation and Dissidence: Hispanic domain*), 1991 and 1994.

IV. *Generaciones y semblanzas: dominio mexicano* (*Genealogies and Biographies: Mexican Domain*), 1991 and 1994.

V. *Sor Juana Inés de la Cruz o las trampas de la fe* (*Sor Juana Inés de la Cruz or the traps of faith*), 1991 and 1994.

VI. *Los privilegios de la vista I: arte moderno universal* (*The Privileges of Sight I: Universal Modern Art*) 1991 and 1994.

VII. *Los privilegios de la vista II: arte de Mexico* (*The Privileges of Sight II: Mexican art*), 1993 and 1994.

VIII. *El peregrino en su patria: historia y politica de Mexico* (*The Pilgrim in his Homeland: History and Politics of Mexico*), 1993 and 1994.

IX. *Ideas y costumbres I: La letra y el cetro* (*Ideas and Customs I: The Word and Sceptre*), 1993 and 1995.

X. *Ideas y costumbres II: usos y símbolos* (*Ideas and Customs II: Usages and Symbols*), 1996 and 1996.

XI. *Obra poética I* (*1935-1970*) (*Poetic Works I, 1935-1970*), 1996 and 1997.

XII. *Obra poética II* (*1969-1998*) (*Poetic Works II, 1969-1998*), 2003 and 2004.

XIII. *Miscelánea I: primeros escritos* (*Miscellany I: First Writings*), 1998 and 1999.

XIV. *Miscelánea II* (*Miscellany II*), 2001 and 2001.

XV. *Miscelánea III* (*Miscellany III*), 2002 and 2003.

XVI. *Obra completa de Octavio Paz* (*Complete Works of Octavio Paz*), author's edition, Galaxia Gutenberg/Círculo de Lectores, Barcelona, 1999-2005; edition in Mexico by the Fonda de Cultura Económica.

XVII. *La casa de la presencia: poesía e historia* (*The House of Presence: Poetry and History*), 1999.

XVIII *Excursiones/incursiones: dominio extranjero (Excursions/ Incursions: Foreign Domain)*. *Fundación y disidencia: dominio hispánico (Foundation and Dissidence: Hispanic domain)*, 2000.

XIX *Generacionesy semblanzas: dominio mexicano (Genealogies and Biographies: Mexican Domain)*. *Sor Juana Inés de la Cruz o las trampas de la fe (Sor Juana Inés de la Cruz or the traps of faith)*, 2001.

XX *Los privilegios de la vista: arte moderno universal (The Privileges of Sight: Universal Modern Art)*. *Arte de México (Mexican Art)*, 2001.

XXI *El peregrino en su patria: historia y politica de México (The Pilgrim in his Homeland: History and politics of Mexico)*, 2002.

XXII. *Ideas y costumbres: la letra y el cetro. Usos y símbolos (Ideas and Customs: the Word and the Sceptre. Usages and Symbols*, 2003.

XXIII *Obra poética (1935-1998) (Poetic works, 1935-1998)*, 2004.

XXIV *Miscelánea: primeros escritos y entrevistas (Miscellany: First Writings and Interviews)*, 2005.

PUBLISHER'S ACKNOWLEDGMENT

Mosaic Press wishes to thank Jeannine Pitas for her tireless work translating *An Introduction to Octavio Paz*. Without her efforts, this book would not have been possible.

TRANSLATOR'S ACKNOWLEDGMENTS

I would like to thank Salvador Alanis for his input in reading and reviewing this translation. I thank Keith Edkins for helping me to navigate through Borgesian libraries of facts and information and for proofreading this text. Brandon Pitts, I am grateful for our literary friendship across time and space. And, most of all, thanks to Howard Aster, Matthew Goody, and everyone at Mosaic Press for offering me the opportunity to do this work.

This translation is dedicated to my esteemed colleagues, Salvador Alanis and Ximena Berecochea, with appreciation and gratitude.